W9-DGC-516

Off the Beaten Path

Off the
Beaten Path

Stories of People Around the World

Ruth Johnson Colvin

Syracuse University Press

Syracuse University Press gratefully acknowledges the generous contribution of the Central New York Community Foundation, Inc., toward the publication of this book.

• • •

Syracuse University Press
Syracuse, New York 13244-5290

First Edition 2011
11 12 13 14 15 16   6 5 4 3 2 1

∞ The paper used in this publication meets the minimum requirements of the American National Standard for Information Sciences—Permanence of Paper for Printed Library Materials, ANSI Z39.48-1992.

For a listing of books published and distributed by Syracuse University Press, visit our Web site at SyracuseUniversityPress.syr.edu.

ISBN: 978-0-8156-0993-3

Library of Congress Cataloging-in-Publication Data
Colvin, Ruth J.
Off the beaten path : stories of people around the world /
Ruth Johnson Colvin. — 1st ed.
p. cm.
ISBN 978-0-8156-0993-3 (cloth : alk. paper) 1. Voyages and travels.   I. Title.
G490.C56 2012
910.4—dc23   2011040058

Manufactured in the United States of America

Dedicated to Bob—
my husband, my best friend, my traveling buddy

Literacy as a global mission has interested **Ruth Johnson Colvin** for years. When she learned that there were more than eleven thousand people functioning at the lowest level of literacy in her own city of Syracuse, New York, she decided to do something about it. In 1962, she started Literacy Volunteers of America, Inc. (LVA), one of the organizations that merged to form ProLiteracy. LVA trained volunteers to teach adult basic literacy and English to speakers of other languages, one on one or in small groups. Mrs. Colvin stresses the importance of a learner-centered, collaborative approach to teaching.

The recipient of nine honorary doctorates, Mrs. Colvin in 1987 was given the highest award for volunteers in the United States—the President's Volunteer Action Award. In 2006 she received the Presidential Medal of Freedom, the highest award that can be given to a civilian. She was inducted into the National Women's Hall of Fame in 1991.

Mrs. Colvin and her husband Bob have traveled across the United States and around the world, visiting sixty-two countries and providing training in twenty-six developing countries. In a richly varied and exciting career, she has found most meaningful the experiences where she assisted and encouraged practical, grass-roots ventures. She continues to work with top professionals in the field, putting the latest research into layman's language and providing how-to teaching techniques.

Ruth Colvin is a living testament to the literacy cause. We were brought together in the 1980s by a mutual passion in life—to educate every man, woman and child. Ruth has compiled inspirational stories from men and women she has met in 26 developing countries. Her passion for literacy has no boundaries and will help people around the world.

—Barbara Bush

Contents

Illustrations

Photographs

Maps

Introduction

This work is not an autobiography, nor is it a travel book. It is a collection of memories of our travels around the world—of people, places, and experiences we encountered that left indelible marks on us. It is a book of stories—the stories of real people whom we met and worked beside in nine countries, of experiences that introduced us to customs and traditions we'd never imagined, of poverty and wealth, of prejudice and service, of unsung and unknown heroes.

Why can't the people of this world live together peacefully? I submit that one reason is that we know so little of one another: of others' histories, cultures, traditions, and religions. In our travels to sixty-two countries, having worked in twenty-six developing countries, we've lived and worked with ordinary people and some who aren't so ordinary, sharing our concerns and interests with them and learning about their diverse and sometimes surprising customs.

In 1995, my husband, Bob, and I were preparing for a volunteer overseas assignment for the International Executive Service Corps (IESC) when we received a phone call from that organization's country director. After exchanging pleasantries, she asked Bob, "Can it possibly be true you'll be eighty years old next February?"

"Why, yes," he told her. "I'll be eighty in February. In fact, we plan to be in Zambia on that birthday."

"I can't believe it. You two seem so much younger. Officially, the cut-off age for volunteer workers is eighty, but if you two are willing to go as co-volunteers, I think I can confirm this assignment."

We were shocked. We were in good health, had talents and skills to share, and had already accepted the assignment. By that time, we had worked in more than twenty countries. We felt that all we had learned from those experiences made us even more valuable to the IESC. As it turned out, we accepted the Zambia assignment that year and have done volunteer work in Papua New Guinea, the Solomon Islands, Cambodia, Madagascar, Guatemala, and Haiti since then. We will continue our travels and our volunteer work as long as we have our health and as long as we are invited.

When did I first wonder about places beyond my own?

As the oldest of five children in a middle-class, single-parent family in Chicago (my father had died suddenly, at age thirty-eight), I was the one who arranged my younger siblings' Sunday afternoon activities. Having exhausted coloring books, games, and stories, I turned to a globe of the world. One by one, we would close our eyes and give the world a spin, then point to one specific spot on the globe. Then each of us would open the *Book of Knowledge* and read all it told us about that spot. With the youthful enthusiasm of a fourteen-year-old, I had promised each of them they would visit that city one day. I remember that *my* city was Hyderabad, India, and I honestly believed I'd travel there. And I did!

Decades later, in 1962, responding first to a local need, I founded Literacy Volunteers of America (LVA; since 2002, merged to become ProLiteracy, with nearly one thousand affiliates). LVA was a national, not-for-profit organization that trained volunteers to teach basic reading, writing, and conversational English to adults who asked for this help. I taught and trained, and I wrote the literacy and English as a Second Language (ESL) books used in our training. As LVA grew, staff and boards of directors took on the leadership and day-to-day work. Meanwhile, I continued researching, teaching, writing, and participating in board decisions.

My first inkling that I'd get involved in international literacy work came in the 1970s, when Dr. Doris Hess, head of the Global Ministries of the United Methodist Church, called and asked me to train Margaret Mujonge of Mozambique in LVA's basic literacy work. Mozambique, an African country devastated by civil war and natural disasters, needed help in basic education for its citizens while it tried to rebuild itself.

I gave a mini-training in basic literacy techniques to both Margaret Mujonge and Dr. Hess and offered them advice on starting literacy programs. That led to our first invitations to India and Africa. I had plenty to learn. For example, the basics can be applied everywhere, but cultures differ and so do learning levels and motivations. Also, some languages are phonetically regular (English is a patterned language but is not phonetically regular). Also, most developing countries do not enjoy the luxury of volunteerism and have to provide most of their teaching in classes—big ones at that. Finally, some countries for political reasons actually discourage basic literacy.

Bob and I began receiving invitations from the IESC, universities, religious organizations, and groups in developing nations asking us to share our skills—Bob's in problem solving in the small business sector, mine in native language literacy and ESL training.

As we met people in other countries, we tried to learn more about them and their lives. We were constantly amazed that people in other countries knew so little of America as we saw and knew it. They knew only what they saw in the movies or on TV or read in their newspapers. For our part, Bob and I knew little about other countries and *their* people, except what we read in *our* newspapers or saw on TV.

I collect people the way others collect stamps or coins. I take great pride and joy in meeting new people, making friends, and learning about their lives, their joys and sorrows, their customs and traditions, whether it be a maharaja, a holy man, or the lowliest peasant of India; an archbishop, a commandant of the defense force, or a Black activist in South Africa. In our adventures, we've found that "people are people" around the world. America has no monopoly in good or evil, but neither does India or Swaziland or China. If the peoples of the world could only communicate as individuals, we would find we have more in common than most of us believe.

How can we understand others if we know nothing of their religious beliefs? Don't three of the major belief systems in this world—Judaism, Christianity, Islam—believe in one God and share Abraham as their "father"? In our years of traveling we have found that many people believe in "one supreme being" with (perhaps) multiple manifestations. Others find spiritual strength in nature and in the wonders of the universe. Still others, agnostics, say "I don't know," while others are atheists, believing that there is no supreme being. Most of us believe as we do because we were brought up that way. What if, just *if,* you had been brought up in another culture, with another belief system? What difference would that make in your life? To live in peace, we must respect others' beliefs or nonbeliefs. We must search out and stress our similarities even while we celebrate our differences.

You, like many others, may not have had the time or the opportunity to travel and work with people in developing countries. Reading about these people is the next best thing to doing that. So come with Bob and me to India, to South Africa, to Nigeria, to Zambia, to Swaziland, to China, to Ecuador, to Madagascar, to Cambodia. Meet the people we encountered as they go about their daily lives. Experience with us the joys of sharing a meal, of meeting other families, of trying to understand other customs and cultures, of helping them whenever and wherever they ask for help.

Come with us on our journeys, for every story is about a journey. Join us as we learn more about other customs, other traditions, other religions. Revisit with us those places where *we* were the minority, not just by the color of our skins but in our customs, our religion, our way of life. We live in a global community, and the more we know about other cultures, other traditions, other experiences, the better we will understand the world.

In these pages you will read about Victor Mitra, a leper in India; Swami Hari Har, the Holy Man of the Geeta ashrams in India; Hemmad and Sheilendra, a maharaja and maharani in Jodphur, India; Dr. Byers Naudi, an Afrikaner in South Africa who worked tirelessly against apartheid; Gugu, a young African rebel who taught illiterate men in a hostel in Soweto; and the seldom-seen Incwala ceremonies in Swaziland. Having read about them, you will, with

1. Ruth and Bob with a map of the places they have visited. Photograph by Nancy T. Stewart.

us, begin to understand the people of the world. Perhaps you will even want to start your own little circle to promote world peace.

James Michener said it well: "If you reject the food, ignore the customs, fear the religion and avoid the people, you might better stay home; you are like a pebble thrown into water; you become wet on the surface but you are never a part of the water."

•   •   •

I can't ever thank all the dedicated, caring people who shared their thoughts, their lives, and their experiences with us as we traveled around the world—heroes and heroines who daily helped others. We are grateful to those organizations and universities that invited us. But also a big thanks to my editors, Mary Selden Evans, Matthew Kudelka, D. J. Whyte, and Kelly Balenske, and to all the Syracuse University Press staff members who shared their talents. Thank you to Gregg Tripoli and Ann Kerr, the "outside expert reviewers"; to Mike Connor, executive editor of the *Syracuse Post-Standard*, for working so closely with me to include those articles first published in the *Post-Standard;* to Peter Allen who made the maps for each chapter; to Dick Sargent for his professional advice; and to Dr. Anis Obeid for insisting this book must be written and for introducing me to the people at SU Press, all of whom encouraged me and made this book more pleasurable to read.

Off the Beaten Path

⬡ India, 1980 and 1982–83

Map of India by Peter Allen.

India! Will it be a land of elephants, monkeys, and snake charmers? Or a land of mystics and sacred cows? Will it be a country of poverty, hunger, and disease? Or a land of fabulously wealthy princes and maharajas? Will India be all of these, or none?

So we were wondering as we started out for several months in India, first in 1980 and again in 1982 and 1983. We found all of those things in some part of India, for India has many facets.

Am I the Daughter of a Hindu Holy Man?

My introduction to India came while we were in Africa in 1977. I had been giving literacy training in Kenya, intending to continue on to Ghana, but because of political problems and the fact that the airport in Ghana was closed for repairs, we had to cancel our visit. We cabled our sponsors in Liberia to say we would be arriving five days early; please meet us at the airport.

On the plane from Nairobi to Monrovia, the capital of Liberia, I was tired. Bob gave me his seat so that I could stretch out, and he sat in the seat behind. Seated to his left was an elderly man with a long red mark on his forehead, wearing an orange robe and sitting in the lotus position, his feet folded under his legs. Bob asked if he spoke English. Yes. Did he want to talk? Yes. Bob learned that his name was Swami Hari Har from India and that he was traveling all over Africa visiting his Geeta ashrams. When the Swami learned that I was doing literacy work, he asked to talk with me. So Bob and I changed seats again.

The Swami wanted to know more about my literacy work. After listening, he told me that when I went to India, I must visit his ashram. Bob and I had no plans to go to India, but I did take his name and address. As we talked, I realized how ignorant I was of Indian religions, but I felt comfortable enough with him to ask what his religion was. He replied: "I believe in the one God."

I pulled myself up tall and said: "I, too, believe in the one God."

"Yes, I know," he said, "for you are my daughter. I've known you for hundreds of years." I hadn't expected to hear that, for back then I knew little of Eastern religions and the Hindu belief in reincarnation. I really was at a loss for words.

Luckily for me, we were nearing Kinshasa, Zaire. The pilot announced that we'd be landing soon and that everyone should return to his own seat, for we'd have a full plane after we picked up the new passengers. So Swami Hari Har and I had no opportunity to continue our conversation. We said our good-byes, hoping someday to meet again.

We arrived in Monrovia about 11 p.m. The airport was tiny, dreary, and dark. As Bob and I went through customs, the officials insisted that we give the address for where we would be staying while in Liberia. We explained that we were expecting someone to meet us and that we didn't know yet where we'd be staying. The officials would not return our passports until we told them. We looked around the airport, hoping someone would call for us, the only White passengers there. But no one was looking for us. I went to retrieve our luggage while Bob returned to the customs official to offer the name of *any* hotel in Monrovia, which was sixty miles away.

While I waited, I saw my friend, Swami Hari Har being greeted by perhaps twenty people, both Africans and Indians, all bowing and placing garlands of flowers around his neck. I knew then that he must be a very important man.

The Swami looked my way. "Are you having problems, daughter?"

"No, no, my husband is taking care of things."

The Swami turned to his aides and said: "That is my daughter. Take care of her."

The next thing I knew, two Indian gentlemen were standing next to me. Bob returned. I introduced the Swami's friends, telling them that all was okay, but the Swami's friends insisted on taking our luggage and leading us to a big, black Mercedes. We found ourselves in the Swami's entourage.

The people in the car were amazed that we didn't know who the Swami was. "He's our Holy Man, head of all the Geeta ashrams in the world." We learned that he was eighty-two years old and that he was making his annual pilgrimage to all his ashrams around the world. Our companions invited us to join them in a worship service in Monrovia. Of course, we accepted, even in the middle of the night. What an invitation!

We arrived at a large, brightly lit house—unusual for Liberia. Entering a room that had a beautiful oriental rug, we removed our shoes, following what the other guests did. They were Africans and Indians, the Indian women wearing colorful saris. Because we were the Swami's friends, we were accepted by everyone.

We were ushered into a small room, bare of furniture except for a low cot on which the Swami was sitting in the lotus position. I wasn't sure what to do, so I stopped at the doorway, looking in. I saw perhaps fifty people—Africans, Indians, men, women, and children—all sitting on the floor, looking up adoringly at the Swami. As each new arrival entered the room, he would walk to the Swami, bow down, and kiss his feet. Now, I've never kissed anyone's feet. This was a new custom for me, and I hesitated to go forward. But the Swami saw my embarrassment and waved to me. "Daughter, daughter," he said. "Come here and sit at my feet."

We became part of the worship service, too. Beautiful singing in Hindi was followed by a short meditation by the Swami in Hindi, translated for us by the Indian hostess of the house. The Swami's message was something like this: "You Africans think God is especially for you. You're right. And you Indians think God is especially for you. You, too, are right. But God is also for my American friends. There is one God over all, to be worshipped and loved by all."

After tea, we realized it was nearly 2 a.m. Quietly, we suggested to our hosts that perhaps someone could take us to our hotel. But no, they wouldn't hear of that. If we were the Swami's friends, we were *their* friends. We were introduced to the Chalappas, who insisted that we come to stay at their home. In fact, they assured us that our luggage was already in their car. Mr. and Mrs. Chalappa hadn't known they would be having houseguests, yet they graciously put up beds for us for the night.

But what had happened to the people who were supposed to meet us? As it turned out, they didn't receive our cablegram until the next morning. When we called in the morning, they were relieved. The cable had said we had arrived the night before. They had called all the local hotels, but we were nowhere to be found. They came right out to get us and to thank the Chalappas for taking such good care of us. But, no, the Chalappas insisted that we were now *their* guests and that we would stay with them the entire week we were to be in Liberia. No matter that our purpose there was working with Christians. In their view, we were helping all God's people. That's international friendship.

To our surprise, in 1980 we *were* invited to India to give literacy trainings in several cities. I wrote to the Swami and received an invitation not just to visit his ashram in Delhi, but to be his guest at an International Geeta Conference in Jodhpur.

Because planes flew only twice a week to Jodhpur, and because we weren't sure what kind of accommodations we'd have (we'd been in many parts of India where facilities were quite primitive), we took only one small suitcase, with soap, towels, and toilet paper, trying to be prepared for whatever situation we faced. We knew there was no alternative—we would have to stay four nights.

Jodhpur is a fair-sized city in western India, right on the Thar Desert, with a modern airport, spectacular flowers, and warm desert winds. We were pleasantly surprised to find the Swami and the conference in a mammoth, brilliantly colored tent over a block long, with thousands of people sitting on the ground, patiently waiting or milling around. We were brought to the Swami, who seemed genuinely delighted to see us again as he gave us his blessing. He suggested we might like to wash up and see our accommodations—the services would start in another hour or so. Hesitantly we agreed. We weren't sure what those accommodations would be, but we told ourselves we could adjust.

Imagine our surprise when we were taken to a magnificent Indian palace, to be the guest of Maharaj Swaroop and Maharani Usha Singh.

The maharaja was the ruler of a district in India; the other men in the royal family were referred to collectively as the *maharaj.* The wife of a maharaja is a maharani, or "rani."

In 1947, when India gained its independence, the maharajas lost all their power but not all their wealth. However, taxes have been very heavy, and the royal families have found it very difficult— often nearly impossible—to maintain their huge palaces. Rani Usha explained that they had converted part of their palace, Ajit Bhawan,

2. Indians waiting for Swami Hari, their holy man, to speak.

into a hotel to help pay its exorbitant expenses. We sipped tea in the elegant courtyard, attended by Indian women in colorful saris and men in bright turbans.

We were brought back to the conference tent, which was decorated with dazzling geometric designs. The tent's size overwhelmed us: more than seven thousand Indians were sitting patiently on the canvas matting that covered the sand. The men sat on the right, the women and children on the left.

I was invited to sit on the stage with the Swami, who was then eighty-five years old. He was dressed in an ocher robe and, as before, had a long red mark down the center of his forehead. Other dignitaries on the stage included the mother of the present maharaja, a charming, quiet but elegant widow, and the Buddhist guru to the king of Thailand. The entire setting was vivid with color—the bright geometric designs of the tent, the colorful saris of the thousands of Indian women, and the brilliant stage backdrop for the dignitaries.

3. *Swami Hari Har, holy man in India.*

The stage backdrop was designed to show the universality of the thinking and faith of those in the Geeta Ashram—one God over all. In the center was a reverse swastika, a Hindu symbol for thousands of years, signifying ongoing life. The Indians were surprised that the swastika disturbed us, as they do not associate it as we Westerners do with the Nazis of Germany. Colorfully displayed were the symbols of other religions—Buddhism, Islam, Taoism, Judaism, Christianity.

Next were prayers, songs, chants, words of inspiration—all in Hindi, occasionally translated for us. As I watched the faces of the thousands of people sitting on the ground in rapt attention, I felt their dedication and serenity. Their history—thousands of years compared to America's mere hundreds—was something I was determined to learn more about. As an American, I had much to learn how these people lived.

Life in a Maharaja's Palace

After the services, as we entered the Ajit Palace, our new home, servant boys in white kurtas and dhotis jumped up to show us our room. They had been sleeping on mats by the door. I woke early the next morning to find the room still dark, for it was draped with heavy gold brocade. Bells pealed out the hour—7 a.m. Sitting in the magnificent courtyard, waiting for breakfast, I looked around. The palace and the courtyard were huge, with hand-laid stone floors, magnificent fountains, shiny brass pots filled with bougainvillea, and intricate tables and lounging chairs.

Someone called out good morning. I returned the call while looking around to see who it was.

"You can't see me," the voice persisted, "but I see you."

It was Usha. She explained that her mother-in-law had lived her entire adult life in purdah (not to be seen by those outside the family). Yet she had also been a sociable and well-educated woman who wanted to know all that was going on around her. So when this palace was built, she had arranged for exquisite latticework to be built into the walls of the second and third floors so that she could see and hear all that went on in the courtyard without herself being seen.

Servant boys with colorful turbans served us breakfast in the formal dining room at a twenty-five-foot table that was dressed with tall silver candelabra and white linen cloths—only for Bob and me. Usha joined us for a cup of tea and to chat. These few days as guests of the maharaja and maharani offered us a glimpse into the glamorous days when royalty ruled India.

We were invited by new friends, Maharaj Himmad Singh and Maharani Sheilendra Singh, to visit the Umaid Palace, which Himmad's father had begun building in 1928. This was the last palace

4. Rani Sheildra, Ruth, Rani Usha, new friends.

built by a maharaja in India. Himmad's father owned thirty-seven thousand square miles, and Himmad remembered parties where they served dinner for three thousand guests. A dome as large as the US Capitol, with a second dome on top (we climbed it by a spiral staircase), covered the entire palace. There were immense courtyards and rooms, astonishing oriental rugs, ornate chandeliers, and magnificent furnishings. In the huge central court was an immense indoor swimming pool.

Because of the tremendous expense just to maintain the Umaid Palace, part of it has operated as a super-deluxe hotel since 1988.

Sheilendra and I had good talks. She was from a royal family, and as soon as she was born, she was given over to an English governess who still, at the age of eighty, was like a mother to her. Her governess now lived with Sheilendra's brother. She had become so Indian that she felt she couldn't live with a "daughter," even though Sheilendra had invited her to do so again and again.

She told me how she was married. Her father had died and her brother thought she should be married (she was eighteen). She thought about it for a week and finally agreed—after all, most of her friends' marriages had already been arranged. The maharaja's family had contacted her family, suggesting that their son, Himmad, was available and interested. Sheilendra quietly asked a favorite uncle to find out about the "boy" (she wasn't supposed to know about him). He checked and said he was a nice "boy." She thought he might be spoiled, rich, and powerful and wasn't sure that was what she wanted. Even so, their engagement was announced. Three years later he came to dinner to meet her and her family. Her brother had taken a picture of him earlier, but she said she "wasn't marrying a face" and insisted she must see him. They were married in the palace, in an elaborate ceremony. The honeymoon? His entire family went with the newlyweds to Bombay (now Mumbai)—and then her new husband was admitted to the hospital—he had measles!

Married women usually have one or two rings on their big and next toes. Some women have a ring on a finger, but usually that is a special gift from her husband, not a wedding ring. All women and girls have pierced ears and wear earrings, and they love bangles—red and gold being the favorite colors. A mother does not come to visit her daughter's home—once married, the daughter is part of the husband's family. So Sheilendra's mother never did visit her.

Himmad told me that his grandfather as a young man was quite a "blade" with the pretty girls. One night he invited several boys to go with him to the fort, where they also invited a "singing girl." Himmad's grandfather's father, a stern old man, found out about it and came storming up to the fort. The boys were terrified and told the singing girl to jump off the wall of the fort, which was at the top of a towering cliff. At the time, a young girl was required to do everything a maharaja or his son said, so she "jumped." The story goes that she was wearing a full skirt that blossomed out like a parachute—and surprise of surprises, she landed on the rocks below and walked away.

Suttee, an Old Custom: Still Alive?

We met more of the royal family, but Himmad Singh and Sheilendra Singh became our special friends, personally showing us around the entire magnificent palace.

As we toured the palace, they told stories about dinner parties for thousands of guests, and Bob rang the five-foot-tall gong. They recounted hunting expeditions as we looked at old pictures and admired stuffed heads of boar, tigers, and elephants.

Looking down at the city from the maharaja's fort, we saw the family's white marble cremation grounds. The custom was that when a man died, he was cremated and his wife could commit suttee—that is, die with him on his funeral pyre. To show that she wanted to do this, the new widow would come to the wall of this fort, dip her hand in vermillion powder, and press her hand on the wall. Later, the outline of her hand would be carved into the stone wall alongside those of other widows who had committed suttee before her. As I studied the handprints of these girls and women,

5. *Handprints of women who committed suttee.*

I was told that according to old Hindu belief, suttee was a special privilege and the duty of a devoted wife.

Sheilendra confided in me that she had witnessed a suttee in 1954—that of her aunt, a thirty-six-year-old woman. Her uncle had been sick for some time, and the family was prepared for his death. All during his illness, her aunt insisted that she would die with him, but the family didn't take her seriously, for they all knew it was not only illegal but a custom that hadn't been followed there for years.

Sheilendra's uncle died, and her aunt, having attended him throughout his long illness, looked worn and haggard. She still insisted that she wanted to die with him. The family sat up all night trying to dissuade her. She would only smile and say: "I'm going to join him." They brought in her children and asked her: "Who will take care of them?" But it was to no avail.

They went to the royal family's cremation grounds on the morning of the funeral, the aunt wearing her wedding sari, looking like a sixteen-year-old bride, her skin glowing and with an otherworldly look in her eyes, quite different from the haggard middle-aged woman of the previous day. The family kept trying to dissuade her, but she sat quietly on the funeral pyre with her husband's head in her lap, smiling with an inner joy. She told her fourteen-year-old son, "Light it . . ." He hesitated. Again, very calmly, she said, "Light it."

It takes at least three hours for a funeral pyre to burn, but the young widow lived only a few minutes. Sheilendra was there but walked away. She felt powerless. She lit a cigarette and pressed the lighted end into the palm of her hand, trying to get the feeling of burning—torture. Unbelievable!

Not too many years ago, traditional Hindus considered her actions not suicide but a holy thing for a pure and devoted wife to do. Changes in customs take time, often generations. Often we do not understand ways that are not our own. But sometimes others do not understand our ways either.

Cremation is the tradition among Hindus. During cremation, all attachments to the spirit are loosed. There are ghats, steps down to the river Ganges. We once saw a big ghat near Kanpur with funeral pyres for ten cremations. We watched while a body (women wrapped in red, men in white) was placed on a pile of wood. More wood was piled on top of it, and ghee—clarified butter—was poured over all. Usually it is the oldest son who walks around the pyre and lights it, but here we saw a priest with a stick of fire circling the pyre, chanting, finally lighting it. It was very simple— done with dignity and prayers. Life goes on.

Travel in India

Indian train stations are always crowded, with people sleeping on the floor with their luggage or boxes. We usually traveled first class, which was far from that by American standards. We always tried to get a compartment, though getting a compartment wouldn't mean being alone. On one train we were surprised to find two strange men in our compartment with us—they had been assigned the upper berths while we had the lower berths. I guess we were just lucky.

On one journey from Delhi to Jodhpur, we found our reserved compartment (always four to a compartment), but there were five men there. We thought we must have the wrong room, but one man spoke some English and explained. Two of the men had reservations; the other three would leave as soon as we wanted to sleep. There was no dining car, and no way to buy food on the train— each passenger has to bring his own—so we had brought oranges, hard-boiled eggs, and biscuits. You don't see the food people bring onto trains until it's time to eat—but food they always have, usually carried in cloth bags.Not sure what to do, we waited and waited. Finally, at 10 p.m., we suggested it might be time to go to bed. I went to the bathroom (only Eastern facilities), and by the time I returned, three of the men had left—apparently they had no reservations and would sleep in the hall. We took off our shoes and jackets, rolled out our sleeping bags, and slept right in our clothes—that's the way it was done in India.

Next morning, not only did the three men return, but so did a fourth passenger. It seems that Indian travelers sense fellow passengers' problems and are polite and invite them to share what-ever space is available.

We had been warned not to open the window while in the sta-tion, for hands will reach in and take anything. As the train sped along, the passengers opened all the windows—better dusty than hot. We had also been warned never to open the door to the train or to your compartment. One night as the train stood in a station, there was a great banging on the door. We sat quietly—no one spoke. A male voice repeated: "Please open up." We waited. Finally the voice spoke in Hindi explaining that he had gotten out of the train in the station to visit a family member in another car, and he couldn't get back in. One brave soul finally opened the door for him, or he'd have been left at the station.

There are dacoits, thieves, who routinely rob trains. While in Kanpur we were told the story of Phoolan, a notorious female dacoit who had recently surrendered. As a teenager, she had been given as a bride to an older man who badly mistreated her. She ran away and was taken in by a gang who raped and tortured her. She fled that gang and started her own, ruthlessly kidnapping, torturing, and murdering others. She was persuaded to surrender in return for leniency. There was lots of publicity!

On our Indian travels, we always carried enough food for the trip at hand, be it for a day or a week. That is how it has always been done in that country—only recently can people be sure of buying food along the way. I can so easily now see the "miracle" of feeding the five thousand as told in our Bible. To me the "magic" of making more fishes and bread seems unlike Jesus. The important miracle was the "changing of their hearts" so that they *shared* the food they had, giving rather than taking. Christianity began as an Eastern religion, and to understand it you must understand Eastern ways.

What Is a "Hutment?"

In India, slums are called "hutments." The largest one in the country was in Dharavi, outside Mumbai. Without Molly, a case-worker, it would have been impossible for us to go there. Indeed, she told us that though she had been there hundreds of times and was well known, she would have gotten lost if she hadn't followed the pipelines.

As we entered the hutment, people stared at us—our white skin, our slacks, and my camera were signs that we didn't belong. We followed the pipelines, which had faucets every block or so, and carefully stepped over the trash and potholes. We were surprised at the cleanliness of the people: they gathered quietly at the faucets, waiting their turn for buckets of water, washing clothes—and themselves—right there.

We visited the Methodist Center, a single tin-roofed room that held perhaps forty preschoolers from 8:30 a.m. to noon. From 12:30 to 5 p.m. there were sewing classes for thirty women, and then from 6 to 8 p.m. children came to study. We visited a house. Six people lived in it, with one bed for the mother and father; the four children slept on the floor. Yet they felt lucky, for they could be together as a family. Even within the hutments, tradition is important, especially when marriages are being arranged. Girls usually marry at age fourteen or fifteen, and so do boys, but often older men seek these younger girls as wives.

A Camel Fair

Pushkar, on the edge of the Thar Desert, is the site of the annual Camel Fair. We went by car with a driver. Most came by bus or camel cart, by bicycle, or on foot. We drove through villages, over rugged mountains, and around hairpin curves, up, down, and around. Hundreds and hundreds of people were walking, walking, walking, for miles and miles and miles.

Among the thousands of villagers, the few tourists lived in tents colored in brilliant geometric designs. Our tent was about twelve by twelve feet, with two cots and a single lightbulb. Austere, yes, but we still felt guilty when we saw the villagers huddled together in small groups by tiny fires. It's cold in the desert at night.

We were up at 5:30, under a full moon and brilliant stars, surrounded by little dung fires lit and silent walking figures, with camels silhouetted against the sky. We joined the jostling crowd, walking toward the lake. The people were in a happy yet serious mood.

The story goes that Rama, the Creator, dropped a lotus flower here in the desert, and water sprang forth where it fell. The result was this dazzling lake in the midst of the desert mountains.

We arrived at the lake and waited for the sun to rise. At the moment of dawn, thousands of tiny clay pots of oil were lit and sent out on the lake as prayers. Above us we saw low-hanging stars. Out on the lake we saw what looked like similar stars—these tiny oil lights—and you sensed the prayers, the thoughts, the dreams of these mountain villagers. In complete silence, we all watched with wonder.

As the sun rose and the lights floated on the lake, activity began. Men and women conducted their ritual ablutions, then drank the holy lake water. Children splashed, enjoying the holiday. One woman walked in waist deep and strewed ashes from a container—probably her husband's.

As we walked back to the fair, we saw snake charmers performing for coins, holy men in ashes wearing only loin cloths, and Hindu priests beckoning the throngs to worship in local temples. The people were eating, cooking, and urinating along the roadside—all natural functions done without embarrassment. There was a festive air, and the villagers were dressed in their very best clothes. The sari-clad women wore all their jewelry—earrings, nose rings, bangles, and necklaces. The Camel Fair was a high point in a dreary, hard-working existence in the villages.

The fair was a gigantic county fair where camels were bought, sold, and traded. There were hundreds and hundreds of camels, the men who owned them huddled nearby with their families. The camel dung had been gathered into piles two feet high. It was valuable as fertilizer, but mostly it was used as fuel in this barren part of India.

For us it was a glimpse into history, for the Puskar Camel Fair had been a highlight for Indian villagers for many generations.

6. *The huge county Camel Fair where hundreds of camels were bought and sold.*

How Father Bede Griffith Brought Christianity to India

Father Bede Griffith, for over twenty-five years a missionary in India, told us: "The early missionaries said they wanted to bring God to India. Does this infer that God had not been in India? It's hard for me to believe that God in His infinite love and wisdom would overlook the millions of people in India over these thousands of years."

He continued: "Our task in India is not so much to bring Christ to India (as though He could be absent), as to discover Christ already present and active in the Hindu soul."

Indians are a deeply religious people. Over 85 percent of them are Hindus. For thousands of years they have searched for truth and God, and they have made a real contribution to Western thought and religions—silence, meditation. While I was seeking to learn more about Hindu thought and worship, I met Father Bede Griffith.

Father Griffith had been educated at Oxford University in England. He wrote in his book *Christ in India:* "As long as we try to present the Gospel message as something *opposed* to the religion and culture of India, we are doomed. . . . When we consider the number

7. *Father Bede Griffith, bringing Christianity to India in the Eastern way.*

of conversions to Christianity in Asia over the last 400 years, we must admit that the Christian mission has largely failed. . . . Why? The Church has always presented herself to the eastern world in the form of the alien culture." Griffith was determined to bring Christianity to India *within* the Indian culture, to emphasize similarities rather than differences.

We traveled fifty-six hours by train to the southern tip of India, to the Shantevanam Ashram near Tiruchirappalli. This Christian ashram, started more than twenty-five years ago by Father Griffith, is set in a typical Indian village, under palm trees by the sacred Cavery River. We lived in his village, participating in the worship services, eating, living with his followers, observing, and listening.

Indian temples and ashrams are colorful, often filled with carvings of gods with several heads and many arms. This had always struck me as unusual until I saw the brightly colored building used for Father Griffith's worship service, with its painted figure at the entrance of Jesus—with *three* heads, representing the Trinity. The Trinity is not difficult for Hindus to accept, for they, too, have a trinity in Brahma, Vishnu, and Shiva.

Visiting here, we lived simply as villagers, sharing the work, sleeping in austere rooms, eating together in silence the plain and nutritious food, washing our own eating utensils, keeping to a schedule of study, work, meditation, and prayer.

At the entrance to the simple, open-sided temple was a large cross garlanded with marigolds, Indian fashion. We removed our shoes as we entered—the Indian custom—and sat on the ground with crossed legs. Bob had no trouble sitting in this position, but my knees wouldn't bend that far, so I sat on the ground in a more comfortable position. We smelled the incense and saw the tiny cups of oil, lighted, to enhance the worship. The Indians were comfortable with this setting, and probably Jesus would have been comfortable, too, with incense and oil lamps.

Bells called us to worship, and more followers quietly entered the temple. Father Griffith and three other white-robed priests sat, lotus position, in the center of this low, oblong building, with the candles, oil lamps, and incense before them. The service opened with the priests and worshippers chanting *ooooommmmmm* . . . the continuous sound reverberating in our ears, letting us zero in on the incense, the candles, and the reason we were here—to worship God. When all felt the oneness, there came the sounds of joy as the priests played Indian string instruments, accompanying the worshippers, who chanted their love of God. Then Father Griffith opened the Bible and read the scriptures in both Hindi and English.

In a short sermon he adapted its message to present-day Indian village life. Singing "Christo Deo Deo," led by Father Griffith, all of us felt the togetherness of India and our own lands as we worshipped the one God. The service ended with the Lord's Prayer in Hindi and with communion.

As Bob and I sat quietly, trying to absorb all they had shared with us, I again realized how much India brings to Christianity—simplicity, silence, meditation, prayer, and joyous praise of God. "Shanti, Shanti, Shanti . . ."—"Peace, Peace, Peace"—the chanting followed us as we quietly left the service.

What Is a "Practicing Hindu"?

Asha and Jeep lived in a tall, elegant building—their home was one entire floor—in Mumbai. Asha told me she was a "practicing Hindu." We often think of Hindus having many gods, but Asha told me that Hindu belief is in one God. He is like a roof over all, and all try to attain Him. There are many ways to reach the roof—steps, a pole, an opening in the roof, and so on. In just the same way, there are many religions.

Hindus also believe in thousands of gods and goddesses, who are manifestations of various personalities or models. You can pick any one of them as your particular model. Asha compared this to Christianity, where one might pick Frances of Assisi, or John the Baptist, as a special model or guru—and pray to him as well. She had a worship room in her house where she prayed.

Jeep, her husband, had picked Krishna as his special god. He used a wooden representation. Asha herself had picked Rana Krishna as hers and used pictures to help her worship.

One devout Hindu explained to us that Krishna is often described as the Supreme lord, but that there are three specific manifestations of the one God—Brahma, creator of the universe; Vishnu, preserver and protector of the universe; and Shiva, destroyer of old and useless things so that new ones can be created.

In another well-educated Hindu family, the wife was a devotee of Krishna, while her husband was a devotee of Shiva. Each had picked the attributes of god he or she admired. One son was quiet and studious—he had picked Krishna. The other son said that Krishna was too calm for him—he was more vigorous and had picked Shiva. The gods to whom they had devoted themselves were models of sorts, guides to what they hoped to become in serving the Almighty.

The Bhagavad Gita, the Hindu holy book, was described to me by a practicing Hindu as teaching that one is born again and again and again until, being selfless, one merges with the Almighty, and that there is only one God, who can be worshipped through any religion.

Hindu beliefs cover a broad spectrum—from a belief in one god over all to reliance on individual manifestations. Religion in India is personal, with devotees attending the temple generally only on auspicious days. Yet there are many tiny street temples where Hindus stop to do *puja* (worship).

The caste system is now illegal in India. Even so, it is still observed, and not just in villages. The castes are still recognized by surnames: Brahmin (priestly) names include Pundit, Swami, and Mudahlian; Warrior (landowner) names include Thakur and Singh; Merchants' names include Jain, Varna, and Madaskwar; and Sudra (artisan and laborer) names, such as Baboram, usually end in "ram." Many Untouchables have converted to Christianity and changed their names.

Hindus call their spiritual leaders by different names. *Swami* is a Hindu title of great respect and honor, given to those who have shown wisdom and spiritual devotion, while a *guru* generally is a personal spiritual teacher.

In India, yoga is often a form of worship as well as of meditation. It refers to traditional physical and mental disciplines. We were invited to be guests of Sri Mahesh Chandra Dwived, a friend's yoga guru. Sri Dwived sat on the floor with his feet tucked under, back straight, his forefinger and thumb touching to make a circle, palms of his hands on his knees, eyes closed, head erect.

After a short prayer, then silence with quiet admonitions to think only of breathing in and out, and a short meditation, the yoga shared his thoughts: "God wants us, like a Father, to take that one step reaching for Him, and He'll take the many steps to reach us. God is within each of us, everywhere. He wants our soul to join Him. Think only of your breathing—in and out—listen to God. His thoughts will reach, will come to you." He talked of Jesus as a perfect example of Oneness with God. One Sunday afternoon we were invited to a *gita satsong*, a monthly gathering of spiritually inclined people, to study the Gita. We joined the twenty worshipers sitting cross-legged on the floor in a small room. In a corner under a canopy were two gods garlanded with incense, joss sticks, and flowers. We were welcomed as "brother" and "sister."

The service started immediately with singing in Hindi, accompanied by a harmonium, drums, and cymbals. This was followed by the reading of a psalm of worship and praise from the Bhagavad Gita. Then more singing and chanting, and finally a social gathering.

People worship a supreme being in many ways. We felt that we were guests in India and that it was only right we visit their temples and learn more about their religion as well as their culture and traditions. We found many similarities with Christianity, and we always respected the differences.

"Temple Babies"?

Calcutta was hot and densely populated. We were near the city center in an old, impoverished area with potholed streets and mounds of trash and rubble. People were sleeping on the streets, and there were hundreds of "pavement children." The parents living on the streets love their children but often can't provide for them. Many children were kidnapped and turned into beggars; many others were living in church-operated schools.

One Methodist worker we met, Karuna Lee, had been a "temple baby." We wanted to know more. We had heard that young girls were sometimes given to the temple and priests to become devotees of specific gods and had unwanted babies, called "temple babies." The story goes that the Lees, years ago, had adopted many of these "temple babies" into their own family, educating and loving them. Who were the Lees, and why had they done this?

The Reverend and Mrs. Lee were Americans working in a Christian school in India in the 1890s. They had six children. One year they returned to Calcutta from Darjeeling, a resort in the Himalayas, having left their children well cared for in that cool, beautiful spot. In September 1899, a landslide carried away their house and all their children, ages three to seventeen. Only one son, a thirteen-year-old, was found to tell the story, but two weeks later, he, too, died. Their entire family was gone in an instant.

The Lees, having a strong faith, decided they would not live a selfish life of mourning. They renewed their work at the school; they also adopted the poorest of their students and gave them the family name of Lee. Today, many teachers and leaders in Calcutta are named Lee, having been "pavement children" or "temple babies." Yet as infants, these people had been wanted by no one.

Leprosy Lives in India

We usually think of leprosy as an ancient disease that has been eradicated. Yet even today, many of India's beggars are lepers. How else could they survive?

Bethany, the leper village near Old Delhi, was for lepers whose disease had been arrested and was not contagious. If their disease was contagious, there were hospitals where they could be treated.

Bethany was set on five acres of land—rock, sand, and scrub, not good for much else. The twenty-two leper families had built their own simple cottages out of clay. Two other of these simple buildings housed looms. Men, often with deformed hands, feet, and faces, sat at the ancient wooden looms, working from dawn to dark. The women spun, sitting on the ground in front of their huts. There was a tiny community building that was a sort of school for the children. When the children were seven, they could attend the Butler School in Old Delhi. Children of leper families do not have leprosy and are not capable of infecting others, but the stigma is still there.

Few people visited this leper village, so the villagers were delighted to see Dr. Rajogopal, our host, and more than pleased to have pictures taken. It was heartbreaking to see faces without noses, hands without fingers, and people hobbling around on stubs. Some had special leather boots that enabled them to walk.

The director, Victor Mitra, a physiotherapist, had had a good education and spoke English quite well. I had heard his story but had forgotten it until I met him and he stuck out his hand to shake mine. He wore a long-sleeved shirt, and naturally I was looking into his eyes as I replied to his greeting. I hope I didn't show my shock, for his hand, when I looked down, had been stiffened by leprosy into a solid, grotesque claw. After a quick shake, I dropped his hand, and we continued talking and walking as he told us about the village.

Victor Mitra was completing his training in physiotherapy when one day, by accident, he spilled boiling water on his arm. Can you imagine his disbelief when he realized that he hadn't felt a thing? The shock he must have felt when he realized *he* was a leper?

Victor had been married, and he and his wife had a son. His wife died shortly after the baby was born. Victor and his son, Andrew, were alone here at Bethany. Victor wanted and needed a mother for little Andrew and a wife for himself. The logical person, in Indian thinking, would be the former wife's younger sister. But this younger sister, Clara, at that time was sixteen years of age, at Butler School, doing well in her schoolwork, and hoping someday to earn a living for herself.

But realistically, what were her chances of getting a job with this limited education? And because she was poor and had no dowry, she had little chance of finding a husband. So it was agreed that young Clara would be given in marriage to Victor, to live with him and Andrew in the leper village.

After a leper's disease had been arrested and he was no longer contagious, he could apply to live in Bethany. He would be given a one-month trial, living right in the village. He was usually accepted if he could show that he could earn his own way and fit into the

8. *Victor Mitra, the director of the Bethany Leper Village and a leper himself, with his wife and son.*

communal setting and that he wanted an honorable living rather than a life as a village beggar.

Victor's story made an indelible print on my mind—real live people were living with the aftereffects of leprosy in this day and age! How would I react if I had spilled boiling water on my hand and discovered I had leprosy? My admiration for Victor grew tremendously; he had chosen to make the most of his tragedy, to be a leader with his son and new wife in Bethany.

Small Clinics, Huge Health Problems

While we were in Delhi, we visited the village of Ganaur with the people from the United Methodist Mission who ran the weekly clinic there. Eleven of us crowded into the clinic jeep for the journey of forty miles, which took over two hours. With us came our own food as well as our own cook, a lab technician who tested specimens with a simple microscope, three doctors, a teacher, and others who helped with nursing and record keeping.

This clinic was twenty-seven years old and was set up weekly in the village compound. Each patient paid five *paeca*, about half a cent. Tuberculosis and polio had been serious problems over the years; but now the main concerns were tapeworm, dysentery, malnutrition, and problems with pregnancy. Family planning was another serious issue: typically, a mother-in-law would insist that her son's wife have many children, who would care for her in her old age. At the same time, the men insisted on more children to help them with the farm work. Infant mortality was high, so families could never be sure how many of their children would live long enough to be useful.

There were difficulties giving medication, for most villagers couldn't read. When giving pills, the doctors often tore two notches on the package if the pills were to be taken twice a day, three if three times a day. But there were still problems. One man was given delousing medication, which he was to put on his scalp. He took it internally instead. Luckily, it only made him vomit.

One girl, a young mother of four, had very poor teeth and was completely worn out physically and emotionally. The doctor suggested she eat porridge. She said she couldn't possibly do that— porridge was *hot,* and this was the *cold* season. How do you combat logic like that?

But good things sometimes happened. One young mother brought in a thanksgiving offering of ten rupees and a small bag of apples. She had had several miscarriages and had not been able to carry a baby to full term. The clinic's doctor, a woman, had worked closely with her, and finally she had carried a baby to full term. Her infant was now five months old, and healthy—quite a contrast to most of the children here, who were tiny, scrawny, and ill. The mother was the biggest advertisement for the clinic. That day she told us she wanted only two children now that she knew how to have them and keep them healthy.

As the women and children waited their turn politely, a teacher took this opportunity to tell stories, emphasizing sanitation. The day I visited, she had a series of pictures about cleanliness. One picture showed a fly, enlarged hundreds of times, demonstrating how it carried germs.

A Baby in Rural India

Dakor is a village of about five thousand people, a Hindu religious center not far from Mumbai. It is extremely poor, and we visited a three-room hut built of mud, dung, and straw that was home to three families.

We met an older woman and two young girls, all dressed in faded saris, each carrying a baby. They showed us their very practical crib. Its four posts and frame were made of wood, but there was no wooden base. Instead, each corner of a square cloth was tied to a post of the crib, making a hammock-like place for the baby to sleep. When the baby soiled the cloth, it could be changed. No diapers were needed.

One woman showed us her baby, at that time over a month old. He had been born with no opening in the rectum. The nearest doctor had told them he wasn't equipped to handle this operation and that they must go elsewhere. They returned to their village—they had no money and no means to go elsewhere—and the baby somehow survived. The mission people found a doctor who might have been able to perform the operation, and they encouraged the parents to take the baby to him. Who knows if the parents ever did.

Infant mortality rates were very high, especially in the villages. How any babies at all survived malnutrition and no sanitation, surrounded by clouds of flies and mosquitoes, is something I'll never understand.

Dakor was a mainly Hindu village, but there was also a Muslim community and a few Christian families. Most Christian families were Untouchables. Their mud-and-straw huts were designated by small crosses over the doorways.

One Orphan's Story: Vanapoo

Vanapoo cooked for us at the school in Madras. She was so responsive to any praise of her cooking, and she tried so hard to please.

In her broken English, Vanapoo told me her story. A poor village man whose wife died in childbirth took his tiny but healthy baby girl to the forest, for there was no way he could care for her. "That was me," Vanapoo told me.

A missionary who worked at a local orphanage, Amy Carmichael, wanted to adopt an Indian baby, but she wanted a *healthy* baby. Her prayers were answered when, walking through the same forest on the same day, she met this man with the baby, who asked, "Please, can you take care of her for me?" Vanapoo knew her father loved her, for even then she was healthy, especially for a girl child. This was a rare thing in poor villages, where girl babies were often abandoned.

Amy Carmichael took Vanapoo to the orphanage, the Dona Voo Fellowship (*dona voo* means "one thousand children"), where she provided special care for Vanapoo for thirty years. When Vanapoo was ten or so she began to help care for the other babies, advancing to jobs of cleaning, sewing, and cooking. She had now been a cook at this school for more than twenty years.

She smiled brightly: "I like it here." Yes, sometimes it was difficult, but she had adjusted. She told me she visited her "home," the orphanage, once a year.

Tragedy in a Marketplace

We bicycled through the streets of Kanpur, an industrial city of more than 1.5 million, about three hundred miles southeast of

Delhi. There were no Westerners or tourists there, so we were a real curiosity as we cycled through streets crowded with bicycle rickshaws, three-wheeled *tempu*s, tooting jalopies, and buffalo. When you're cycling in traffic—and that's nearly always—you learn to identify who's coming up behind you: a bell for a bicycle, a continuous bell for a rickshaw, a sort of buzzer for a scooter, a horn for a car, a special horn for a *tempu*—and when one hears a *loud* horn, it's a bus or truck, and you get out of the way at once.

Sometimes you see huge elephants lumbering down the main streets, carrying loads. No one pays attention to them. Cows wander freely, for Hindus consider them sacred. Even city people own cows, and while they're producing milk the owners keep them carefully close to home. When the cows go dry, the owners can't afford to feed them and turn them loose to find whatever food they can, knowing there are always scraps in the streets. Owners can identify their own cows, and when it's time to breed them, they again keep them close to home.

We learned to maneuver around the cows, but one day, three cows were walking down the road at least five feet from me. As I passed, one must have kicked the other, for it charged at me. I

9. *Fun times as Bob pedaled me around in a local rickshaw.*

dodged back, and it missed me by a hair. A bit unnerving—you have to have strong nerves and quick reflexes to survive in Kanpur.

We were invited to Hudson School in Kanpur to give literacy training. There were more than eight hundred students at Hudson, which was sponsored by the Global Ministries of the United Methodist Church. Hudson was an austere-looking place, but by Indian standards it was deluxe. There was hot water, but that meant only that a bucket of water was brought to you: you were expected to warm it up yourself with a coil heater. And yes, there was electricity—but that only meant that lights and wiring had been installed. One never knew when the electricity would suddenly go off, which often happened in the middle of a training session. There was a telephone, and perhaps it would be working, though even if it was, the one you were calling often wasn't. If you wanted to talk to someone, it was usually easier to hop on your bike, even if it meant a half-hour ride each way.

There was always dust and wind. The people worked hard sweeping the paths and roads, but that labor was never ending. Many women we saw were permanently bent over, their backs parallel to the ground. They were the sweepers, who used short, short brooms. I never could find out why they didn't have longer handles.

You constantly heard beggars wailing "Memsab, Memsab." They would follow us, their disfigured part uncovered: a boy with a stub of an arm at the shoulder, another boy with an elbow heavily bandaged, yet another who was blind, women with babies covered with scabs. One boy was wearing an old bandage that he had obviously dipped in something red to look like blood. He confirmed for us tales that the beggars were organized. Indeed, sometimes they even kidnapped people and disfigured them on purpose to generate more sympathy. We were advised not to give them money and to ignore them. Even so, they tore at my heartstrings—you feel so helpless.

In the colorful street markets, where fruits and vegetables were beautifully displayed, you were expected to bargain. Produce spoiled quickly in the hot sun—no refrigeration here.

Eileen, an Indian nurse at the Hudson School, did most of the marketing for the school. She knew when fruits and vegetables were in season, which ones were of good quality, and how much to pay. Indeed, she knew most of the market people.

One day she saw a young mother holding her baby. The baby's hand and arm seemed attached to the baby's face. Looking closely, Eileen saw that they *were* attached. The mother told the story.

The baby had been lying on a cloth next to a box that held a small kerosene lamp of the type used by most street people. The mother left for a few minutes to run an errand. A gust of wind toppled the lamp, burning the baby. The tiny girl didn't cry much but kept her arm up to her face. Now the skin had grown together.

Eileen was aghast. She put the mother and baby in the school car, and off they went to a doctor. A minor operation separated the cheek and the arm, leaving ragged scars. But the little one survived.

As I looked at the little girl, knowing her story, I wondered about her future. Would it be fairly normal? Hardly. A Hindu girl with scars on her face and arm is hardly a candidate for a good marriage. There was no chance for an education for any of the street children. I hesitate to put into words what her future life was going to be.

A Lifetime of Service: Lillian Wallace

The missionaries I saw in India were not trying to change Indian ways to Western ones. They were quietly helping people—Hindus, Muslims, and Christians—setting an example by *living* their Christian beliefs. Schools, education, helping Indians help themselves—that was the focus.

Lillian Wallace, director of the Hudson School, had been a missionary in India for over thirty-five years. She was a remarkable woman who lived an exemplary life as she helped Indians.

Hudson School was for poor families. Educating their children has always been a high priority for most Indians, but even the very low fee of four dollars per month at Hudson School was out of reach for most families. The head of a family whose children were at Hudson often earned between twenty-five and thirty dollars per month.

A high percentage of the children at Hudson were being subsidized by American and German donors.

But Lillian Wallace let the "ripples from the pebbles she dropped" go beyond her work at the school. She often saw individual children who fit into no category and who needed help.

One such girl was "Little Ruth," called that because she was so tiny. Little Ruth wasn't the brightest child, but she was a loving, helpful youngster who grew in helpfulness even while she didn't grow in size. Even in her twenties, Little Ruth was a bit over four feet tall.

Little Ruth's parents died when she was a child at Hudson. Her four older brothers simply disappeared. So Little Ruth became another personal charge for Lillian, who always insisted that you must pass on the good things that come your way. In the end, Little Ruth became an auxiliary nurse serving faraway villages.

Before you hear more about Little Ruth, you should know the story of Lavinia and Renuka.

Lavinia was at the Hudson School hostel, sponsored by an American family who paid the four dollar monthly fees and additional monies for clothing and supplemental food. No one was sure of Lavinia's age; she was probably seven or eight, but oh so tiny, even for that age. Lavinia had watched her father die in a fireworks accident. Shortly after that traumatic experience, Lavinia was swinging on some wires that held a brick wall at the hostel. The wall collapsed on her, pinning her to the ground. Both her legs were fractured, and the calf muscles were torn out, leaving a huge gap in one leg. She was given up for dead several times, but somehow she survived. She could still walk, but her legs were deformed and a mass of scars.

And Renuka, Lavinia's tiny sister, was five years old but so frail she looked like two or three. She had been overlooked in all the trauma of Lavinia's life, living quietly in her sister's shadow in the hostel.

Let's return to Little Ruth, the village nurse. She had heard about little Renuka, and she returned to Hudson to meet her. With no fanfare or explanations, she decided to sponsor little Renuka, giving four dollars of her meager forty-dollar monthly wages. She had taken Lillian Wallace's message to heart. She knew she had to share with others who were needier than she.

That was the spirit at Hudson School in Kanpur: *pass it on.* Much had been given to each of them, and now their responsibility was to help others. Drop your pebble. Don't try to find it and save it for yourself. Let the ripples go on and on and on.

Lavinia and Renuka

It was a Hindu holiday, and all the children in the hostel at Hudson had gone to be with their parents except two, Lavinia and Renuka. Their mother was a loving mother. Having had no education as a youngster, she had worked hard to learn on her own. She worked twelve hours a day as an auxiliary nurse, earning forty dollars a month. This barely took care of her own needs and was not enough for her children. She hadn't the time or the money to visit Lavinia and Renuka often, but she continued to work toward the day she could visit regularly.

The girls felt deserted, even though Lillian had explained to them how much their mother loved them and how hard she was working to make life better for them. The first day they were alone—two little girls in a room with eight cots, the other girls having gone—both girls stayed in bed all day, and Lavinia wouldn't eat, withdrawing from all of us.

Lavinia's sad expression reminded us that she relived her father's death in nightmares and often cried all night for her mother. And Renuka leaned on her big sister for support. In spite of all the tragedy, with the love and support of those at Hudson, we knew that Lavinia was a survivor, that she'd make it.

"Uncle Bob" and I spent as much time as we could with Lavinia and Renuka, playing games, giving hugs. It filled us with joy to see their eyes sparkle—they needed not only love but also approval and success in even the simplest games. It nearly broke our hearts to think of them alone each night, missing their mother, just waiting for their classmates to return.

Little Ruth's Village

Little Ruth had become an auxiliary nurse, assigned to ten remote Hindu villages as midwife. She earned forty dollars per month, barely enough to support herself. Her work was difficult, for she was the only nurse and the only Christian in the area. She invited Bob and me to spend four days with her in her villages, walking the long roads with her while she cared for the sick and helpless.

We were up at 5 a.m., rushing to get to the bus station. There had once been fixed times for the 'battered old bus to her village, but no more. Little Ruth found our bus and loaded our two sleeping bags, a smaller bag, water, and a bag of food. We sat, waiting; the bus wouldn't start out until it was full. Meanwhile the driver was out brushing his teeth, carefully avoiding two cows lying on the street next to his bus.

After nearly thirty miles of rough roads to the next village, we, with our luggage and twelve others, piled into a *tempu,* a three-wheeled vehicle. Fifteen miles an hour felt like sixty on the pot-holed roads, as we picked up three more passengers (though there was seating for only nine). At yet another village, we left the *tempu* and carried our belongings to another bus. Yes, and then waited and waited again for the bus to fill. We finally arrived at Ruth's village, Shahelpur, shortly before noon.

Ruth served ten villages, but Shahelpur was her base. It was small and very primitive, with some brick buildings but mostly mud huts, and three wells for different castes (one caste will not drink from the same well as another). Her house, provided by the government, was somewhat better than most, with two small rooms, one for sleeping and the other for cooking. There was one Eastern toilet (hole in the floor) in the corner. In little niches in the wall were two glasses, two plates, two saucers, a knife, a tiny mirror, a small kerosene stove, two small pots, a basket, and two pails for water.

Water first—we let down the pail on a long rope into the local well to pull up our water. Our first meal in Shahelpur: flour mixed with water to make *chapattis,* which we topped with the peanut butter and jelly we had brought. A walk to two nearby villages to make house calls gave us an opportunity to see the tiny but clean huts and meet the villagers. For dinner, hard-boiled eggs (brought by us—there were few eggs in the village because the people were vegetarians) with bouillon soup, then to bed by 8 p.m. Bob and I in our sleeping bags on the *charpoy* (cot), while Little Ruth slept on top of the table.

Bob was up at 6 a.m. to go to the fields for his "morning call." He later confided to me that he was embarrassed because he found that's when all the women go to the field for the same reason. He tried hard to be discreet.

A boy came by to make a small fire of twigs in a *chula* for warmth. A neighbor came by with milk fresh from her cow, and another brought us *shuka kandee* (sweet potatoes). Visitors kept coming, curious to see us. They were amazed by the two-way zipper on Bob's jacket, and everyone watched as he shaved—one young man wanted to try it, too. Little Ruth warned us to eat a good breakfast because we'd probably have no lunch.

We walked with Little Ruth to another village to make house calls: a weary pregnant mother with too many children already, a young man with malaria, children with malnutrition—the needs were endless. Quietly, Little Ruth continued her work—she had found her niche in the world, giving and sharing, passing on some of the gifts that had been given to her.

The Teachers at Hudson School

The teachers at Hudson were all Indians and taught in both English and Hindi. One special young teacher was Madhu Dan. Madhu, in her mid-twenties, had been orphaned early and brought up by relatives. She was dark-skinned, quiet, sincere, capable, and hard working.

Madhu was married. She had lost her first baby more than a year earlier and was pregnant again. Because of her past experience and present complications, she knew this birth would have to be

10. All the teachers at Hudson School were Indians, proudly teaching in both English and Hindi.

by Cesarean section. Government hospitals and medical treatments were free, but they were not set up for unusual cases. Lillian had arranged for a private gynecologist to do the Cesarean section.

We all expected Madhu to have her baby during the Christmas holidays. However, Madhu and her mother-in-law showed up at Hudson the first day *after* the holidays. Madhu was already in the early stages of labor. But Madhu knew that government regulations would allow schools to give holiday pay *only* if the teacher was present the first day *after* a holiday. Madhu needed the money and insisted on coming to school in a crude rickshaw that very day, even as her labor pains advanced.

We tried to telephone her doctor, but the phone wasn't working. So Lillian put Madhu in the back seat of the school car. The car's battery was always low, and it had to be pushed each morning to get it started. No exception today. The men working on the school grounds were called. They pushed. But the car hardly moved. Someone noticed a flat tire!

Imagine—a woman in labor who should have a Cesarean. The phone not working. The car battery dead. A flat tire. Everyone jumped into action. Within five minutes, the tire was changed and we were off. I went with Madhu to the government hospital while Lillian went off in a bicycle rickshaw to try to find the private doctor.

The government hospital was old, dirty, and disorganized. People wandered in and out. We signed Madhu in at the front desk and were told to go to the labor room. We wandered around, asking, and finally found it. A nurse took Madhu's papers and assigned her to a bed, one of about twelve in the room. There were no sheets on the bed, but Madhu lay down, pulling her shawl over her. The nurse returned to take Madhu's history and temperature. I was nervous, but Madhu was calm.

I looked around. All but two of the beds were occupied. Some of the women, like Madhu, were in labor, but there was one woman who had just given birth. The baby was only a half-hour old, and baby and mother were just lying there on a cot, covered with an old sheet, waiting to enter the hospital ward.

The gynecologist came. A Cesarean was performed, and a little girl was born. Madhu and her little one were rolled out of the operating room on a rusty cart, Madhu covered with her own shawl, the baby wrapped in some of the used clothing and blankets she had brought. By this time, her husband had found us, with a friend. He, the friend, Madhu's mother-in-law, and I followed Madhu and the baby in the cart as it was pulled to the hospital ward.

As we stood at Madhu's bed, waiting for her to awaken, I reminded myself where we were—in a hospital in India. I knew no Hindi so I couldn't communicate with the others. I couldn't help but think of my own daughter's care and attention when our grandchild was born. I became a bit angry—we are *not* created equal. This little one certainly wouldn't have the same care and opportunities as my grandchild. But she would have the same motherly love.

After two days, Bob and I got on our bicycles, carrying gifts for the new baby, and pedaled to the hospital, only to find that Madhu and her daughter had gone home the day before. How? In a bicycle rickshaw, of course!

The school knew that Madhu had moved but didn't have her new address. After much detective work, we found it and went to visit her. Most streets in Kanpur were crowded and littered, and Madhu's street was no exception. In an old wooden building, we walked up three flights of dark stairs and found Madhu and her mother-in-law and the baby. They were delighted to see us and showed us "Pinkie," the new baby. The three of them, as well as Madhu's husband, who was a welder, lived in this one room. There were no bathing facilities. Water was carried upstairs in a pail.

Madhu's mother-in-law was the perfect Indian hostess, boiling water over the charcoal fire to make tea for us, their special guests. I was honored, for Madhu insisted that I hold the new baby.

Hindus will not enter the room of a new mother until her baby is a month old. But the one Christian neighbor came in. The others peered in the doorway, curious to see us, Madhu's American friends.

When Madhu was teaching she made about thirty-five dollars a month. Madhu's husband made about the same. Food took 80 to 90 percent of their income. Rent necessarily was very low—probably four dollars a month for this one room. After clothing, furniture, utensils, and medical supplies, there was nothing left. Even so, Madhu felt lucky, for they had two incomes—admittedly not always steady. She knew she would be able to teach her own daughter, and she hoped that Pinkie would be able to attend Hudson School, that perhaps someone would subsidize her. Education for their children continues to be the highest dream for most Indians.

There were some outstanding hospitals in Kanpur. McRoberts Hospital, across from Hudson School, was one of them. McRoberts was a private hospital with lovely grounds. Its rooms and offices were austere but immaculate. At the time Madhu gave birth, a room there cost 120 rupees ($12) a day, which was beyond the reach of most Indians. Dr. Bhatnagar, who ran McRoberts, was British trained and a member of the Royal Order of Physicians. He had been a teaching doctor in one of the top medical schools. Now he wanted to show by example that India could provide top-quality medical care, and he provided that in his own hospital.

Sharing among the Poorest

Indians are a religious people and generally accept the inclusion of Christianity in the curriculum of Christian schools. Although Hudson was a Christian school, perhaps four-fifths of the children were Hindus, all of them from very poor families. Because education is one of the greatest gifts that Indian parents can give their children, even the poorest parents will sacrifice to get their youngsters into a school. India's public schools were very weak academically, and most private schools were expensive. The parents' only hope was to have their children accepted at one of the Christian schools. The fees at Hudson were low, yet many parents could not pay even those. Perhaps one-fifth of the students at Hudson, from these poorest of the poor, were sponsored by the Christian Children's Fund (CCF).

It was December 1982. The Hudson School family—teachers, servants, students, and families—had gathered for the annual Christmas party.

The CCF children had practiced and practiced for this first presentation of the Christmas story to their parents. For this special occasion, the entrance to the small building used for student gatherings had been decorated with *rangoli*—traditional Hindu designs made with rice powder.

About two hundred parents arrived, dressed in their best but a bit hesitant, for all of this was new to them. The women and girls sat on the floor on the left side of the hall—eager yet shy, expectant yet wary. The men and boys sat on the right, a little more confident.

The lights went out, and there on the stage were about fifty tiny clay dishes filled with oil and burning brightly. You could hear the "ahhh" from the audience. This was familiar. This they knew, for oil lamps are used for Divoli, a special Hindu festival. A graceful

11. Hundreds of parents sat quietly on the floor, waiting for the celebration, the first time they'd heard the story of Christmas.

young girl did a Hindu dance around the oil lights, followed by some of the CCF mothers from the sewing group, dressed in their finest saris, singing in Hindi.

Next came the Christmas story, in Hindi. The CCF children were dressed in homemade costumes. We couldn't understand a word of Hindi, but we knew the story well—Mary, Joseph, the angels, the shepherds. The parents were entranced, and not a sound was heard.

Then the three Wise Men brought their gifts. Everyone froze while a short announcement was made, in Hindi, to the audience. They had been told that there would be an opportunity to share, but no one knew how these Hindu parents would react. The announcement in Hindi went something like this:

> How fortunate we all are. Our children are in school, getting a good education. But we are even more fortunate for we have *love*—parents loving children, children loving parents. We want to share with those who have less than we do. There are unwanted babies right here in Kanpur who have no *love*. We will bring the

12. *The Christmas story was told in Hindi, as the children acted it out for their parents.*

gifts of the Wise Men from the people here at Hudson to Mother Theresa's Home for Children. If any of you have anything you, too, want to share, do come forward and leave your gifts at the foot of the Baby.

The parents had been told they *could* give to the unwanted babies, and they were prepared. The entire audience rose at once, carrying tiny packages wrapped in old newspaper, a few coins. These were the very poor families of Kanpur, so poor that their children's education was subsidized by Americans, but they, too, wanted to share with those who had even less.

The next morning Bob and I joined those from Hudson, together with two Hindu parents and several CCF children, to go to Mother Theresa's *sishu bhawan,* Home for Children, to share the love and also the gifts with the little unwanted ones. We saw and felt the love and care given by the Sisters of Mercy as they prepared the unwanted babies for adoption or for some future life.

But after half an hour, the sisters said they were sorry but they had to be on their way, for they, too, needed to share what they had received. They were going to the hutments, the slum areas, to give a party for the pavement children. "Freely we receive. Freely we give."

The Americans shared by supporting the poorest children in India through the CCF. The parents of these children who had so little but did have love to give their own children, shared with those who had even less—the babies who were unwanted, unloved. And the Sisters of Mercy, caring for these deserted little ones, shared with the pavement children. That's the true spirit of sharing.

South Africa, 1978, 1983–84, and 1988

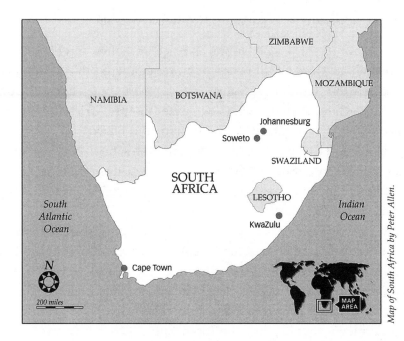

Map of South Africa by Peter Allen.

Africa, the "Dark Continent," brings to mind lions, giraffes, elephants, impalas, wildebeests, and thousands of wild animals. But what about the Africans themselves? When Bob and I first traveled to Africa in the 1970s, few Americans knew much about that huge continent's history or people. Few Westerners visited, and those who did typically went on safari to the game farms.

In the 1970s and early 1980s, the Global Missions of the United Methodist Church and the International Executive Service Corps invited us to Africa to give literacy training workshops in several countries. We weren't sure what we'd find, but because we would be working with Africans themselves, trying to share what skills we had, we knew we would see parts of the continent that few tourists see.

Since then, Bob and I have visited sixteen African countries and worked in ten of them. I have stories to share about people in four African countries: South Africa, Nigeria, Zambia, and Swaziland.

My Introduction to Apartheid: Kathleen Manual

Most of us think of Africans as Black and often forget there are also "White Africans." It needs to be remembered that White people ruled the Republic of South Africa for many decades through their apartheid system, which separated South Africans into four unequal groups: White, Colored, Indian, and Black.

I had read *Cry, the Beloved Country* in high school, but I had never met anyone from South Africa. So when Kathleen Manual visited our church in Syracuse, New York, in the late 1950s, I couldn't wait for her to tell her story.

Kathleen looked "white" to me, for her skin seemed no more than healthily tanned and her features were Caucasian. From that, I assumed I would hear the story of South Africa from the Afrikaner perspective. I needed the balance after reading the story of the Black pastor in *Cry, the Beloved Country.*

Kathleen was born in Cape Town, South Africa. She was "mixed race," mostly White but probably with a Black somewhere down the line. But there came a time in South Africa when all people had to register themselves, and each had to register as White, Colored, Indian, or Black. Those four groups were to be divided in terms of where they lived and went to school and what jobs they could take. Kathleen, clearly, had a difficult decision to make.

Because of her light coloring and Caucasian features, she would have been able to "pass"—that is, declare herself White. There were advantages and disadvantages. If she registered as White, she'd have to give up her family and friends but would be able to live and go to school in a White district. If she declared herself Colored, she could remain with her family and friends but her education and job opportunities would be limited for the rest of her life. It was a difficult decision, but her family would support her whichever way she decided.

After much prayer and hard thinking, she opted to register as Colored, and when she visited us, that was how she talked about her life in South Africa. She described the mediocre housing, the weak education system, and the limited job opportunities and pay available to Colored South Africans, whose status was less than that of Whites but higher than that of Blacks.

George Manual, her husband, was a light cocoa color. He was a writer and journalist and had received many awards from the Cape Town mayor for his work on the local newspaper. Yet he was paid less than his White colleagues. And when a young White reporter was hired under him, the young reporter's beginning salary was higher than what George Manual was receiving after twenty years. These were the things that hurt. He knew it was unfair, but what could he do?

I corresponded with Kathleen and George for over twenty years, never expecting to see them again. Then in 1978 I was invited to several African countries by the Global Ministries of the United Methodist Church to give literacy training. One of the countries would be South Africa. Of course I wrote to the Manuals, hoping to visit them.

In Cape Town, we were staying at a very nice hotel. I called Kathleen, inviting her and her husband to be our guests for dinner. She suggested that we come to their home instead. I insisted—I wanted them as *our* guests. "Wouldn't you like to see a Colored neighborhood?" she replied. "To see where we live?" Yes, indeed, I would, so we accepted their invitation to dinner.

The Manuals lived in a modest but fairly modern house in an unpretentious neighborhood. She and George showed us where the borders of their township were, explaining the apartheid concept of separate housing areas. Kathleen's daughter, Lorna, was a teacher in the Colored schools. She was not quite as docile and accepting as her mother and father were. She explained that her classes were larger than White classes, that not all her children had books as they did in White schools, and that the pay for Colored teachers was lower. "It's not right," she insisted, and I agreed—to which her mother softly countered: "But it's better for us as Coloreds than it is for the Blacks." Kathleen's daughter agreed with that. Her friends who were Black teachers were paid even less, had had less schooling themselves, faced larger classes, and had even fewer books and teaching materials. That was how it was in South Africa in 1978, even in Cape Town, which was far more relaxed than Johannesburg.

Not until later did I realize that Kathleen had invited us to her home because she knew that she and George wouldn't be welcome at our hotel. Most of the hotels were for Whites only. Only one or two of the very top hotels were "international," meaning that international guests of color were welcome.

It's different being right there, not merely reading about it, knowing that you must consider a person's color before you can invite someone as your guest. I would not have been able to stay overnight in her home, either—I was the wrong color. And the laws were even stricter in Black townships. I had been born White, which meant that in South Africa, certain rights were my "due."

Literacy Training Workshops Make a Difference

Apartheid. I had heard the word, but I had no real idea of what it actually meant until we visited South Africa in 1978. I soon learned, once I saw signs saying "Whites Only" on certain benches in downtown areas. "Non-Whites Only" was on specific buses or toilets, and many restaurants displayed "Right of Entrance Reserved" signs. There were designated areas for "Coloureds," others for "Indians," and still others for "Blacks."

Apartheid is an Afrikaans word that was used for almost forty years to signify "apartness" or "separateness." Obviously, separateness—*apart-heid*—did not mean equality, for Bob and I soon realized that we would need police permission before we could visit or work in non-White areas.

I had given literacy training workshops in other African countries, but in the Republic of South Africa I could see and feel a *separateness* instead of a *togetherness*, even among Christians, for most of South Africa is Christian. The White Afrikaners identified with Abraham from the Old Testament and believed they had been chosen by God as the superior race. For their part, Blacks quoted the New Testament in support of their right to equality with Whites.

Our colleagues seemed hesitant to talk except in hushed voices about *where* we should do the training. Finally, it was arranged for us to meet at a suburban White church, a traditional-looking building on a tree-lined street with a basement for meetings and suppers. No police were around, but the feeling of apprehension was always there.

All groups were included in my literacy training. Those who attended knew this was "illegal." But I soon realized that Blacks, Coloreds, Indians, and Whites continued to meet and work together, especially in church settings, though always quietly. At the time, I didn't realize how big a risk these people were taking just by meeting together.

One of the attendees was a soft-spoken Black woman, Leah Tutu. This tall, stately woman taught sewing, cooking, and literacy to Black women, who desperately needed those skills in order to find jobs in the White community. Yes, she was the wife of Bishop Desmond Tutu—but even she was only one person, doing what she could.

It was during our second visit to South Africa—in 1984, when apartheid was in the international headlines—that I really experienced the separateness of the races. The South African Council of Churches had asked for my literacy workshop. Literacy workers in the South African Defense Force, in the Hartbeestfontain Gold Mines, and in the Black homelands also wanted my training. Would it be possible for me, an outsider, to get these people with opposing political views to meet? The South African Council of Churches and the South African Defense Force represented warring factions. Confrontation had often brought bloodshed.

Listening to my inner voice, I approached the South African Council of Churches, asking whether these outside organizations could send representatives. Their first reaction was "impossible," but prayerfully they reconsidered. It was Bishop (later Archbishop) Desmond Tutu—Leah's husband, who was later awarded the Nobel Prize for Peace—who heard me out and agreed to extend the invitation. In part, this was his way of underscoring his belief in the equality of all South Africans, whatever their color. Without Bishop Tutu's efforts, I would not have been able to give this training.

Hosting my literacy training was the South African Council of Churches in Johannesburg, whose offices had been raided by the police many times. Security there was tight, and there was fear in the air as the training approached.

But the day came, and the heads of literacy programs in the South African Defense Force, the Hartbeestfontain Gold Mines, the South African Council of Churches, and the Black homelands sat with people of Soweto, a Black township. They were all there for the same reason—to learn how to teach others to read.

There was tension, and then apprehension, when introductions were made during that first workshop session. One gentle Black woman, furtively looking at the military, whispered to me: "Do you realize what you're doing putting all of us in the same room?" I hesitated, for I wasn't sure either. Why had that inner voice encouraged me to include everyone?

But a small miracle happened. By focusing on our common concern—the need for practical and professional literacy training—all of the participants worked together, supporting and encouraging one another. The tensions evaporated.

During the last session, a young Black adult educator from Soweto, acting as teacher, and the White commandant of the South African Defense Force, acting as student, role-played a lesson. It was obvious they had learned to respect each other, for they demonstrated a teaching session in Zulu, which both spoke. Applause

13. A young Black educator, acting as teacher, and a White commandant of the South African Defense Force, acting as student, role-playing a lesson.

from the group showed appreciation not only for the work done, but also for the cooperative effort of people from opposing political groups.

Would this be a step toward reconciliation? Had these sessions made a difference? Did working together on a joint problem help change apartheid to togetherness, even for a very short time? I want to believe that it did.

Whites Working Against Apartheid: The Randalls

You've all heard about Archbishop Desmond Tutu and Nelson Mandela, Black people of South Africa who campaigned against Apartheid. But did all Whites support the Apartheid system?

No, they did not—many Whites were against apartheid, and you can imagine how their lives changed when their friends and colleagues began harassing them for their beliefs.

Pieter and Isobel Randall were fourth-generation South Africans. They had two children, ages eighteen and twenty-three. They were liberal, English-speaking South Africans. Pieter, a university professor, was the owner of Ravan Press, Isobel was editor. The entire Randall family believed in equality of the races and had been vocal, through their publishing company, in telling of real-life situations in South Africa, expressing their disapproval of the apartheid system.

What a shock it was to them when, in October 1977, a police officer came to their door late at night, bringing with him a banning order on Pieter. There was no warning—the ban was to go into effect immediately. Pieter could not go to the university. He could no longer run his publishing business. He could meet with only one person at a time and could not attend any meetings. He could go only a limited distance from his home. He was not told what charges had been laid against him, and he was to be entirely at the government's mercy for the next five years.

Can you imagine destroying a man, his business, and his life at the stroke of a pen? The Randalls sold the business to raise funds to live on. Isobel continued as editor and took a full-time teaching job. In 1982, when the ban was removed, Pieter returned to Witwatersrand University as professor, but the Randalls' phone continued to be tapped, and they were watched closely.

Isobel wrote a book called *Thula Baba*, which means "Don't Cry, Baby." It was an account of domestic workers—poorly paid, unskilled Black women. Most of these women "lived in," separated from their families. They not only ran White homes, cleaning, cooking, washing, ironing, and shopping, but also took care of the White babies, acting as their "nannies" as they grew up. Many "Madams"—that's what the White women were called—were considerate, but many were demanding and treated their "girls" as almost subhuman.

After our Sunday meal together, Isobel had invited five Black domestics from the Centre of Concern to talk with me. These five had been selected to go to America for special training in household skills, so that they would be able to train rural women. They wanted to meet some Americans, to hear more about what they could expect in America. All spoke English and Afrikaans as well as one or two Black languages. They all realized how dependent their White families were on them. Each had been with the same family for over twenty years.

Sophia Nyathia, a Zulu, had been with one family for twenty-two years. When their house was sold, the price of the house included Sophia's agreement to stay on with the new family. She stayed six years, until the lady of the house died.

Centres of Concern had been started by liberal churchwomen in South Africa years earlier to help Black domestics. Both Blacks and Whites took leadership roles. By tradition, Thursdays were "maid's day off." And what did these live-in domestics do and where did they go on their only day off so far from home? They were invited to the church for tea in the morning, with an all-day program, including lunch and training.

Education and practical skills were keys to moving upward. But before Blacks could move upward, the ties of apartheid would have to be broken.

An Unsung Hero: Dr. Byers Naudi

One unsung hero, Dr. Byers Naudi, was truly a man of faith, who put his beliefs as a Christian into action.

Dr. Naudi, when I met him in 1978, during the worst years of apartheid, was in his sixties. He was married and had a grown family, and he was a minister of the Dutch Reformed Church, an Afrikaner church whose members absolutely believed that they, the Whites of South Africa, were God's Chosen People.

Dr. Naudi at one time had been president of the Broderbund, a secret brotherhood of Afrikaners, whose members included all the key figures in the South African government. Over the years, Dr. Naudi had searched his heart, trying to uncover what God and the Bible really were telling South Africans. Was it truly God's plan that

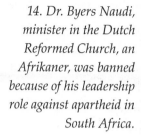

*14. Dr. Byers Naudi,
minister in the Dutch
Reformed Church, an
Afrikaner, was banned
because of his leadership
role against apartheid in
South Africa.*

the Whites—especially the Afrikaners—were His Chosen People, a Master Race whose responsibility was to help the others?

As Dr. Naudi met with leaders of the Blacks, the Coloreds, and the Indians, he came to see the inequality those groups faced. He began building coalitions in an effort to find a better solution than apartheid. But the Afrikaners, especially the leaders of the Broderbund, wouldn't budge. Finally, in desperation, after much prayer and soul searching, he opened the secrets of the Broderbund so that everyone would know the beliefs and plans of the Afrikaner leadership.

What a shock to the nation! His actions made headlines; everyone was talking about them. Dr. Naudi was ejected from the Broderbund. The government couldn't jail him, for he had broken no laws, but they did something nearly as severe—they "banned" him, just as they had Pieter Randall.

Ken, a South African friend who knew Dr. Naudi, called him to see if he'd meet me. Yes, he would be delighted. So on a Saturday morning in April 1978, Ken drove me to Dr. Naudi's home in a Johannesburg suburb. I assumed that Ken would go in to introduce me. But no, Ken had to wait in the car, for one of the restrictions placed on Dr. Naudi was that he could see only one person at a time.

Dr. Naudi was a tall, poised, self-confident yet humble man who greeted me warmly. I introduced myself, offering good wishes from his friends in the United States, especially those in the United Methodist Church, and gave him a brief description of my work.

I asked many questions, though I wouldn't be permitted to share our conversation with others. I could tell friends casually about our visit, but I couldn't talk to a group—that would have violated his ban, and he would have been punished for it. He could leave his house, but only during certain set hours. He could never meet or talk with more than one person at a time. His wife couldn't even have tea with us, for their house was being closely watched and government agents could enter at any time to punish him.

Just as he was telling me that, his wife, Elsa, came in to ask if we'd have tea. I was so afraid of doing something wrong that I replied I was just thrilled to be with her husband, no, thank you. Dr. Naudi said *he* would have tea and asked me if I was sure I wouldn't. Well, I figured, if he was, I would. And his wife brought tea in, but only *two* cups—one for him, one for me. No, she couldn't have tea with us, for that would have been considered a small group.

I asked if he could go to church—remember that he was a minister in one of the largest Afrikaner churches. Yes, he could go to church, but he had to sit alone and talk to no one. He couldn't have tea with the parishioners after the service. If he met a couple on the street, and they came over to talk with him, he had to remind them that he was "banned" and that he could only talk to one of them. He was living like a leper from biblical times, having to call out "unclean" when people came near.

On top of that, he was forbidden to communicate with other banned people, who included most of his friends and colleagues. His phone was tapped, so the apartheid government always knew who was calling and what was being said. They also knew everyone who visited him—yes, I would be on their list now, too.

I asked if he was doing any writing, for he had been a prolific writer. No, the ban forbade him to write. I couldn't understand how he could keep up his spirits—perhaps he could just write for himself. No, he said, the government would have considered that "planning for publishing," which was also forbidden. Yes, he could read—that was a saving grace. But reading was giving him only the news the South African government wanted him to read.

How did he earn a living? What could he do when he could see only one person at a time? Some people in his church were offering financial support, and one local church had agreed to have him do counseling. But as he pointed out, most problems arise because of *two* people's needs. However, he did counsel people each morning, though only one person at a time.

I asked how those in the United States could help. He asked that we pray for South Africans and try to understand their real problems. He told me it was nearly impossible for the outside world to see the real situation, for the South African papers could only publish the government side. He felt that most reporters wanted to print the truth. Unfortunately, when a story was published saying anything at all critical of the present government, that newspaper was shut down immediately.

The week before this meeting, I had met a young South African who knew Dr. Naudi. When he heard I would be seeing him, he quickly wrote a note, asking me to give it to him. I wasn't sure what to do. If I was searched—which was quite possible—and the note was found on me, I wasn't sure what would happen to me. I hadn't brought a purse or anything that looked suspicious—only a pad of paper and a pen. I had hidden the letter under the belt of my slacks. Now I turned away and took the paper out, telling him I'd met a friend of his who had given me this letter. Dr. Naudi was delighted, read the letter quickly, and said he'd destroy it.

Our hour together went quickly, I felt honored and humbled to have spoken to this dedicated Christian.

Apartheid was the legal system in South Africa for forty years, from 1950 to 1990, when it was officially ended. For twenty-five of those years, Dr. Naudi had the courage of his Christian beliefs; he met with leaders of other races in defiance of the law of South Africa, to work toward reconciliation, even to defy his own church's beliefs and expose the secrets of the Broderbund. For that, he was banned for fifteen years. He was the strongest dissenting voice among the Afrikaners, putting his Christian beliefs and his strong faith into action. Dr. Naudi died a few years ago, but he lived to see the apartheid system end.

Gugu: A Revolutionary Hero

In 1977, industrial leaders in South Africa, realizing that the present government would never make the necessary reforms, and Clive Mennel, chairman of the board of Anglovaal Ltd., one of South Africa's largest mining companies, spearheaded a gathering of concerned industrial leaders. These leaders decided to form the Urban Foundation, funded by themselves, whose major concerns would be housing and education for Blacks as they fought for equality and change. One of the Urban Foundation projects was Funda Centre, an educational centre in Soweto that trained Blacks to help others in their community.

I heard about a young radical, GuGu Ngeme, who worked with the Funda Centre, teaching literacy in the single-sex hostels of Soweto. Someone had suggested to GuGu that he meet me, but he wasn't sure he wanted to work with a white American woman. He came to my orientation anyway, and we hit it off. He asked whether he could send six of his young Black teachers to my training.

My mental image of a young Black "radical" was of an arrogant, defensive young man who was anxious to fight, to pillage, to take

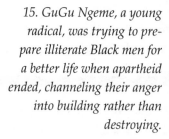

15. GuGu Ngeme, a young radical, was trying to prepare illiterate Black men for a better life when apartheid ended, channeling their anger into building rather than destroying.

revenge on his oppressors. But GuGu didn't fit those preconceptions. He was a gentle young man, reserved and polite, yet firm. He was from Natal, a rural area. He had graduated from college with a degree in biology and animal research. In 1976 he came to Johannesburg and got a job, but he had no "pass" and was jailed for two months. Another job, no pass, arrested again. Then he met men working to help Blacks in the Funda Centre in Soweto.

Remarkably, GuGu had built a literacy group with limited facilities, few books, and no training. He repeated his theme to me again and again: prepare the men for a better life when apartheid ends; channel people's anger into building rather than destroying.

I included GuGu's six men with other trainees in my literacy workshop in Johannesburg.

Zakhele was a young trainee who had been teaching at the Funda Centre. Zakhele's father lived in another hostel as a migrant worker. When Zakhele first came to Johannesburg from Natal, he slept under his father's bed at the hostel, always wary of police raids. GuGu found him and placed him in a Salvation Army hostel with the other young teachers. It was clean and safe there, and they had a place to cook.

Jabu Mbotha was twenty-three, from Natal, a Zulu. He had two brothers and two sisters. His mother was a domestic in Johannesburg. His father was unemployed in Natal and taking care of the family. His family was very poor, he said. He had come to Johannesburg for the holidays to look for a temporary job, for if he wanted to get his high school diploma, he would have to raise the money to school himself. He did get his diploma, and he felt lucky to be working at the Funda Centre to help others with their basic education.

GuGu knew the anger and frustration of men like these—he felt it, too. But for him the answer was not demonstrations, street battles, hatred; it was *building* his community in preparation for the day apartheid ended.

Gugu and my six young trainees invited me to the tiny chapel in Soweto where they taught. I was so proud of "my young men," each in a corner quietly teaching from ten to thirty men. I had wondered why these young men were sometimes late to my training and often tired, but soon I understood. They often rose before 5 a.m. to walk to the train station to get the train from Soweto to Johannesburg for my training. They'd do the required homework in the afternoon and return to Soweto to teach from 9 to 11 p.m. These were dedicated young men, but they needed the "how to" skills of teaching. Where could they, as Blacks, acquire those skills in South Africa? GuGu told me that these hostel men were at the bottom of the ladder. Even the township people scorned them. He insisted they must be helped, and he had enlisted my aid.

The Mosalas: How One Family Beat the System

I first met Bernadette Mosala in 1983 when she traveled through the United States, representing the South African Council of Churches. It was through Bernadette that I gave that first workshop in South Africa. When I returned to South Africa for three months in 1988, we met again.

Bernadette, a Zulu, and her husband, Leonard, a Sotho, lived in a lovely, comfortable modern house in Soweto, but behind high walls and a locked gate. Both were well educated, as were their two daughters. Donata had graduated from Grinnell College in Iowa, and Carol was assistant administrator at Bernadette's new school. As was traditional in African culture, extended families were always made welcome. When we visited, a niece was living with the Mosalas. There were always relatives who needed help.

Leonard worked in the personnel department of a large company in Johannesburg. He was also an anti-apartheid leader in Soweto. Blacks in South Africa were never completely safe from the government. Bernadette and Leonard had both been in jail many times. Their house had been raided repeatedly, their phone tapped. They tried to keep a low profile, for they were honest and hard working, however strong their anger and frustration with the system.

When we were there, their daughter Carol's fiancé had been in jail for over eight months. He had been driving home to Soweto when he stopped to give a young man a lift. The police stopped him and found guns in a brown bag. The hitchhiker insisted that it wasn't his bag, that it had been in the car before he got in. Carol's fiancé had never seen the brown bag before he picked up the young man. The police didn't know whom to believe, so both young men were imprisoned, and under Section 29, Carol's fiancé had been forbidden visitors. Carol, Bernadette, and Leonard faced this stoically: it happened *so* often. They could only wait, perhaps one more month, for a trial. I never did hear the outcome.

Bernadette clung to traditional customs when it came to their young people getting married. No matter that Bernadette was Zulu—because Carol's father was Sotho, Carol was Sotho as well.

Bernadette described the tribal traditions. When young people decide to marry, the boy's family sends representatives to meet the girl's family and discuss *lobelo*, the bride price. The terms are traditional—twenty cattle, ten sheep, four goats—even though the *lobelo* is paid in South African currency (the rand). The boy's family pays the *lobelo;* in return, the girl must be prepared to start a home and a family. Even in the late 1980s, when a Sotho was married, it was customary to slaughter an animal.

Bernadette said that another tradition was for the boy's family to give the bride's mother a three-legged pot. She insisted that this be done—she *wanted* the traditional pot. South Africa was modernizing, yet traditions like these lingered, giving a sense of continuity to life.

Bernadette dreamed of having first-rate education for all students in South Africa, but being Black, she knew that was impossible. Well, nearly impossible: she had started her own school, the Educational Programs Center (EPC), where there was no discrimination. Most of the 350 students were Black, but there were some Colored and some Indians. No Whites had applied. She had circumvented the law requiring that schools be registered with the government by saying that EPC was not a "school" but an "education center." No "teachers," she insisted, just "tutors" who helped the students. Up until then she had encountered no problems. She insisted on the highest educational standards, believing that education is key to the future of Black South Africans.

Bernadette, when she launched her school, was forbidden to use the White educational standards, but she refused to use the Colored, Indian, or Black standards. She came up with an ingenious plan: she'd use the British standards as supplied to her through the British Embassy. Those were comparable to the White standard in South Africa, and the government couldn't stop her. Even better, the British system was accepted by the universities and big industry. Yes, Bernadette had found a way to play the system.

Fear and Surveillance

Because of our work with the South African Council of Churches, which was highly active against apartheid; my visits to Archbishop Tutu, Dr. Naudi, and Isobel and Pieter Randall, who had all been banned for years; and our work with the Read Educational Trust and the Black reformers in Soweto, our friends assured us that the South African government had a file on us. It was very likely that the phone at our hotel apartment was tapped.

Phone service in South Africa was excellent, but I noticed a definite difference in quality when I talked with the Randalls, who were under surveillance, and again when I received a call from Washington, DC, from our son.

One day there was a knock on the door of our apartment. When I answered, the man said he was the phone repairman. I told him there was nothing wrong with our phone. He insisted there was something wrong with the connection between our room and the conference center. Was I being paranoid, or could it be our phone was being tapped? I watched carefully while he fussed with the wiring. He insisted that all was okay. But you can be sure we were very careful what we said on the phone and in the room.

We were staying at an integrated hotel. Most of the guests were White, but some were Colored, Indian, or Black. The management was White, but most of the workers were Black, and we became good friends with most of the Black staff. *They* knew what we were doing, for they were the ones who cleaned up, set up our equipment for training, and served the tea. One morning we found scratched on the mirrored wall of the elevator the words, "Kill the Whites." Feelings ran high.

All may have seemed calm and open in South Africa, especially in the White areas. But there was a constant undertow of fear. Heather, one of the secretaries, showed me the gun she kept in her handbag at all times. She assured me it was legal and that many White women kept these tiny deadly weapons within easy reach.

What Is a Homeland?

In 1970 the Bantu Homelands Citizenship Act became law in South Africa. This act stated that every Black South African was a citizen of one of the "homelands," no matter where he happened to live. This homeland citizenship made little difference in 1970, for each Black person was then also a citizen of South Africa.

The big change came when some homelands decided to claim independence. Between 1976 and 1981, when four homelands made that choice, eight million Blacks lost their South African citizenship. The South African government's thinking was that if there were enough independent homelands, the percentage of Black South African citizens would decrease, as each Black South African would become a citizen of his particular homeland instead of being a South African citizen.

Homelands were lands near areas where Black tribes had once lived that were being bought up by the South African government from White owners. In most cases the land was of poor quality. The White farmers wanted to keep the rich farmlands along the rivers. Much of the time, the parcels of land for individual homelands were not even connected. I visited two of these homelands.

KwaZulu

I was invited to KwaZulu by Dr. Dhlomo, its minister of education and culture. KwaZulu is the homeland of the Zulus, the largest Black tribe in South Africa, with more than five million people—more than the four and a half million Whites in the country. KwaZulu comprised six separate parcels of land. It had chosen not to accept the independence that the South African government had offered it, declaring instead that its people were South Africans who should not have to give up their South African citizenship.

The Zulus were constructing new government buildings in Ulundi, the capital of KwaZulu, but progress was slow because of lack of funds. Much of the KwaZulu land was of poor quality. When I visited, there had been a drought for more than two years. Rivers had dried up; water shortages were severe. It was depressing to see prosperous White farmland between the Zulu parcels. Afrikaners told me that the government was trying to buy more land from the Whites to give to the Zulus, who faced long odds to make a living from their fields.

There had been no way for me to reach KwaZulu except by bus, which was for Blacks only, or by private car. Dr. Dhlomo had sent a car and driver for me. The four-hour drive gave me an opportunity to talk with a Zulu. Let me share his story.

Thanduxolo Nyawo was thirty years old, was married, and had a six-year-old daughter. He told me he was Catholic, then added that many African Christians were becoming doubters because Christianity clashed with Zulu traditions. But he felt that one could be a Christian as well as a good Zulu.

Thanduxolo told me about witch doctors. He said there were two kinds, the *inyanga* and the *sangoma*. The *inyanga* were there to help and heal, using trees, roots, animals, bones, seawater, and skins to heal people physically and mentally. The *inyanga* were very powerful. If you wanted someone killed, they could do it. He had seen one *inyanga* witch doctor put paint on the wheel of a car. The next day that car overturned and the driver was killed. He told me the *inyanga* weren't always good people.

But most Zulus went to *sangoma*s for help. If you were in trouble, or were sick, or had a purse stolen, perhaps your forefathers could help you, but they couldn't communicate directly with you, only through the *sangoma*. The *sangoma* had supernatural powers.

I asked Thanduxolo if he had ever been to a *sangoma*. Yes, he replied—many times. The year before, he had had severe stomach pains, and for six months he couldn't find work. He went to a *sangoma* to learn the cause. This *sangoma* was a woman, and she told him his forefathers were complaining. Since leaving school he had forgotten them, and he had done nothing to say "thank you" to them. The *sangoma* suggested a village feast.

Thanduxolo searched for a goat and killed it. He and his friends then made Zulu beer, and he invited the people in his village to a feast. The results? His stomach pains had disappeared, and he found this driver's job.

Thanduxolo also told me about the African custom of *lobola*, the bride price, slightly different for each tribe. It was felt that a young man should have as many women as possible, the better for him to choose his wife. This meant that young men and women in his village often slept together. When a young man fell in love, he had to decide whether to marry.

However, if the girl he was sleeping with got pregnant, there was trouble. Whether or not they were married, the boy would have to pay half the *lobola* or bride price. The young man would get the baby when it grew up, but the mother would be responsible for raising it.

If the young man decided to marry the girl, and if she agreed, he would ask one or two men in his family to go to the parents of the woman and tell them that he wanted to marry their daughter. The prospective bridegroom could not go himself. His family members would negotiate the *lobola*.

A normal *lobola* was eleven cattle, unless the girl was the daughter of a headman; then the price was higher. Thanduxolo paid eleven cattle for his wife. He didn't have the actual cattle, but the price of cows was the basis for negotiation. The price of one cow was two hundred rand (at that time a rand was about a dollar), so he had to pay about twenty-two hundred dollars. He had married his wife three years earlier, when his daughter was three. They had had a Christian church wedding, then returned to Zulu customs for the festivities, dancing and beating drums for joy, celebrating with families and friends.

According to Zulu custom, a man could have as many wives as he could support. As a Christian, though, Thanduxolo could have only one wife. Most Zulus have only one, except for their king, who had three wives.

The Homeland of Bophuthatswana

I was invited to Bophuthatswana, the Black homeland of the Tswana tribe, which claimed 2.5 million people. The Republic of Bophuthatswana attained its independence in 1977. It is a nonracial country—that is, it has White as well as Black citizens—and comprises seven separate parcels of land. Bophuthatswana is *not* recognized by other countries (including the United States),

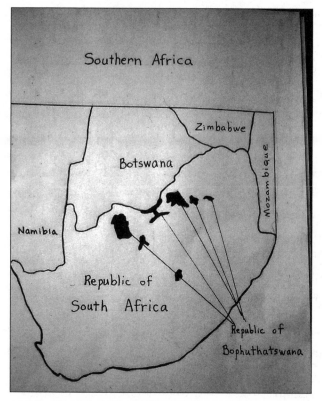

16. *The Black homeland of Bophuthatswana was divided into seven separate poor parcels of land.*

mainly because most countries were against South Africa's apartheid system. Few people know much about the Republic of Bophuthatswana.

Because I'm American and because the United States does not recognize Bophuthatswana, I approached the US Embassy in Pretoria for advice. There I was met by an attractive and self-confident young American woman. When I explained my plans, she had some suggestions. For example, when we came to the border of Bophuthatswana and they asked to see my passport, I should instead give them some other ID—perhaps my driver's license.

"But what if they insist on seeing my passport?"

"Well, show it to them, but ask them to stamp on a separate paper."

"But if they insist on stamping my passport?"

"Well—let them, but also let them know that America does not recognize their government."

I decided I'd carry my passport, but around my middle under my blouse and slacks. And I'd have my driver's license available in my bag. I felt I was at least doing what my government wanted.

Dr. Holele, minister of education of Bophuthatswana, sent a driver and Baratang (Connie) Thetele, an education officer, on a five-hour drive to get me. Baratang was a Tswana, and while she was in the United States in 1977 her people had elected to take the independence offered by the South African government. Knowing that it wasn't fair and that the seven separate parcels of land were undesirable, they still chose independence.

She told me that Bophuthatswanan officials had not stopped trying to negotiate a fairer settlement, but they had decided not to waste their energies on more hatred and fighting. They realized that the South African government was strong and that changes might not take place in their lifetimes. They had chosen to channel their energies into positive building, to show the White South Africans that they were not only equal but superior and could make a model country out of nothing. Most of the government ministers I met in Bophuthatswana were well-educated men in their mid-forties— capable, not bitter, and committed to their people, their country, and their dream. I even had an audience with President Mangope, a quiet, serene man who I immediately felt could be trusted.

Baratang was a tall and very attractive Black woman who had been twelve years in the United States. Her husband, like many Black intellectuals, had simply disappeared in South Africa some years before, and she had gone to the United States to complete her education. She had earned two master's degrees and completed almost all of her doctoral dissertation. Then she learned that her husband had "surfaced" in South Africa but was in critical condition. He died. Baratang returned to South Africa to bury her husband. She wanted to return to the United States to complete her doctorate, but the South African government would not renew her passport. She was disappointed, even bitter, but after a year of soul searching, she decided she would not spend the rest of her life's energy on dreams that might not come true in her lifetime. She decided to become a citizen of Bophuthatswana and was assigned the post of education officer.

I learned all of this and more as she and I traveled the several hours to Mmabatho, the homeland's capital. Halfway there I told her what the US Embassy had told me—and that even if I produced my driver's license at first, I did have my passport with me. She laughed. "Just wait," she told me.

By the end of our five-hour drive, we had become good friends. Suddenly she told me, "You're in Bophuthatswana."

"But where is the border? Why didn't they check on me?"

There was no formal border—no sentries. It was like entering and leaving an American state. The young woman at the US Embassy had known nothing about the reality of the borders. I was sure she had never been there, and I wondered if anyone from the US Embassy in South Africa had ever been to Bophuthatswana. Was it possible that I knew more of what was actually happening there than our own embassy?

Honored Guests in Bophuthatswana

Honored guests are treated extremely well in Bophuthatswana. I was housed in Mmabatho's one hotel—a beautiful place. I was invited to give a one-day literacy training seminar. Teachers were brought in from the neighboring districts, dressed in their best and excited. They were open to new ideas and responded with enthusiasm.

Bophuthatswana had come a long way in the past few years. I saw very poor neighborhoods where corrugated shacks had been raised to house families that had been displaced into this home-land. Many of the shacks were in poor condition, and people were still coming. But I also saw many houses where bricks had

17. Ruth greeted by the president of Bophuthatswana.

been added, trees planted, small gardens started, stucco painted on. And I saw large, lovely homes where people lived well. This seemed to be a democratic country where there were opportunities, and people were being encouraged to support their country. But because the United States did not recognize the government of Bophuthatswana, little help was coming from outside.

Where could a new, poor country find the money to pay for its people's education, health care, water, and other necessities? Bophuthatswana had elected to develop Sun City, a resort area that would be open to the rich Whites in South Africa as well as to Indians, Coloreds, and Blacks. Revenues the government drew from the gambling casino there would be invested in Bophuthatswana.

Sun City was being built on one of the land parcels on the South African border, two hours from Pretoria. It was an oasis in the midst of barren countryside, with swimming, sunbathing, eating, relaxing, golf, and tennis. It's an example of what can be done when finances, determination, and hard work are combined.

Repression and Prejudices

There seemed to be some acceptance of Blacks by Whites in big cities, but in rural areas, some Whites hated the Blacks and really were fearful of equality of any kind. Let me give one example.

While I was returning from Bophuthatswana with Baratang and our Black driver, we drove through lovely countryside. We had had a fine trip and had met outstanding people.

Suddenly Baratang and the driver spoke in Sitswana. They drove into a gas station, looked around, and drove out. I couldn't understand what they were looking for. Finally I asked, "Don't they have the kind of gas you want?"

Baratang explained: "No—we're looking for toilet facilities. Some gas stations only have facilities for Whites, and I'm not permitted to use them. But I'm getting desperate."

In the South African village of Zeerust, we found a Mobil station that usually had restrooms for Blacks. We stopped and looked. There was a room that said "Ladies" and another that said "Gents." Baratang explained that all South Africans know that Blacks are not considered "ladies," but she couldn't wait any longer. I suggested: "Let's go together."

The door was locked. I said I'd go for the key, and she decided to look in another door in the back. Maybe that one was for non-Whites. As she looked in the door, she called out that it was only a storeroom. I decided to take a quick picture of her by that door.

A fat, unkempt White man came running from the station toward me, hollering, "What are you doing?"

I was surprised, but answered, "I'm taking a picture of my friend."

He came up close to me and shouted, "You know you can't do that! This is private property!" He shook his fist at Baratang, screaming, "And *you!* You know you're not supposed to go there! Why did you do it?"

Baratang calmly said, "I needed to use the facilities."

I was frightened, but Baratang just took my arm and said, "Let's walk away—come on."

The man came after us, hollering, "You can't take a picture! This is private property!" I became a bit braver and replied, "You mean I can't take a picture on private property?"

"No!" Arm in arm, Baratang and I walked quickly to the car. She cautioned me to be quiet. She said that if I were Black and had talked back to him he probably would have slapped me.

As we drove away, I told myself I should have turned my camera on him and taken *his* picture. By that time my fear had turned to fury—I was *mad.*

Baratang and Petsi, our driver, assured me that this behavior was typical in many rural areas. Even in cities, middle- and lower-class restaurants were still separated. Only the expensive ones were "international," accepting Blacks.

⊛ Nigeria, 1991

Map of Nigeria by Peter Allen.

*An earlier version of this article appeared
in the* Syracuse Post-Standard *on May 2, 1992.*

Nigeria, with more than one hundred million people, is the most populous country in all of Africa. The Hausa people inhabit the north, the Yoruba the west, and the Ibo the east. Nigeria is a religiously diverse country: Muslim, Christian, and animist. I was invited to present a paper, telling of my literacy program in the USA, at a World Literacy Conference in Ibadan, Nigeria.

"Better Life for Rural Women"—and They're Doing It Themselves

At first, I wasn't sure I'd heard correctly: Did Ibadan, Nigeria—a huge city—have an aluminum factory run by women? I had my doubts, especially when I was told it was one of several hundred projects launched by Better Life for Rural Women. When Rahamat Adisa, wife of the military governor of Oyo, the largest and most powerful state of Nigeria, invited me to visit five projects run by the program, I eagerly accepted.

An official escort van led the way, its blue lights flashing and sirens screaming, carrying two armed guards and cameramen. Mrs. Adisa and I followed in another car, our driver weaving through the dense traffic to the distant rural area where the aluminum factory had been built. While we rode, Mrs. Adisa explained the Better Life for Rural Women program.

For hundreds of years, African women did most of the work in the fields, in the home, and in the market, bearing too many children and with little hope for the future. In 1987, just five years before my visit, the women of Nigeria united under their nation's First Lady, Mrs. Maryam Babangida, to take their lives and their children's lives into their own hands. The Better Life for Rural Women movement was born.

Under the program, women who wanted to participate formed rural cooperatives of fifty to one hundred volunteers. When they had registered with the Better Life program and chosen a project, they could ask for a small loan. The money came directly from local bankers, who soon saw that these were safe loans. They charged very low interest, with the expectation that the loans would be paid off within six months. Each co-op was free to sell its products and keep the profits to repay the loan and to set up an account for its next project.

The first project we visited was for making flour from cassava, a white root that is grown in abundance in Nigeria. Instead of grinding it by hand, the women wanted to buy a simple grinding machine.

They formed and registered their co-op, got their loan, purchased the simple machine, and were in business, quickly making a profit. They invested the profits in their next wish—a ten-foot-long metal tray under which they could build a fire for quick-drying the flour from the cassava mash. Diligent work and good marketing led to steady profits.

The women needed to be able to read and write in order to keep their accounts. This generated a need for literacy classes—the second project I visited. Eight women, colorfully dressed in native costume—including the *gilli*, the famous headdress, made by winding yards of cloth around the head—sat at old, child-size desks in a simple schoolroom. They repeated the exercises, rote-style, while the teacher taught them the same lessons she gave the children. The women were determined to learn and, I was told, came day after day. They sang a song in their native language, which was translated for me: "I will not give up, I will not give up, I will go on until I learn to read and write." An inspiration indeed!

The third project was a simple batik project. The leader, who knew the process, took great pride in her students, who at first followed only her designs but soon became creative, making original designs as they dyed the local cotton fabrics in huge open barrels.

At the fourth project I visited, six women were working at tiny, five-inch looms, hand-weaving yards and yards of colorful, beautifully patterned fabric strips. This project and the batik one provided material for the local women's clothing, but international markets had been found for the fabrics as well.

But it was the fifth project, the aluminum factory, that intrigued me the most. Had the women previously worked in an aluminum factory and brought the skills home? No, they said, they had started out knowing nothing of metals or molds. They only knew they needed sturdy, round aluminum pots for their own use. The co-op had assigned two of its members to visit an aluminum factory in the city for two weeks and learn all they could, then return to teach the rural women. They found that they could make pots with only primitive equipment: a mud outdoor oven, a sturdy nine-inch container for the molten metal, and a simple sand mold. The women scoured the district for old cans and aluminum scrap metal and were soon in business, making pots one at a time, and making money.

One hitch soon arose: the owner of the tiny, dark building where they poured the molten metal wanted to raise the rent. The women found vacant land nearby, bought cement blocks with their profits, and built their own space. I saw their nearly completed building, which was being constructed entirely by the women (and, yes, their husbands). They were already planning their next project—acquiring a simple machine to process and store palm oil.

Just five years after the Better Life program was launched, hundreds—perhaps thousands—of Nigerian women were showing by their actions that they could "do it themselves." They were becoming successful entrepreneurs and were proud of their accomplishments. They knew they would have to be able to read, write, and compute if they hoped to care for themselves and their families.

What about the men? I was told that the rural men were jealous, asking when there would be a "Better Life for Rural Men." The women responded, "We've done it ourselves. You do it yourselves."

I couldn't wait to add these experiences to my conference notes. In the countryside just a few miles from Ibadan, I had seen examples of women's literacy programs and community development in action, as advocated by those attending the World Conference.

④ Zambia, 1978 and 1995

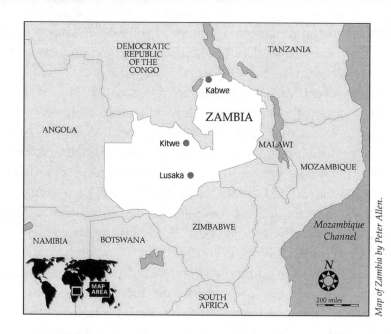

Map of Zambia by Peter Allen.

Zambia is a landlocked country in Central Africa. I had first visited in 1978 and noticed its unmet needs for family planning and "health literacy." In 1995, after years of dictatorship, Zambia had elected Frederick Chiluba as president. The people were jubilant, believing that now they would have more opportunity to open small businesses. But few people had business experience, and the remainder were testing uncharted waters.

At the IESC's invitation, I traveled to Zambia to start a basic literacy project, working with the minister of education. Bob was assigned to advise five small businesses.

74

Family Planning, 1978

Margaret Mutambo, with the YWCA of Zambia, was an enthusiastic trainee in my literacy training workshop. She was pretty, soft-spoken, and highly capable. She had seen the need for literacy through her work with a family planning agency.

Margaret explained that family planning was no problem in the villages, where it had been done in traditional ways for generations. Each village wanted to grow and have more people, but the elders knew how many people their village could feed. Also, the elders were concerned about the health of mothers and their children and knew that having children too close together was bad for both mother and child.

By tradition, the father had his separate hut, and mother and father did not sleep together again until the youngest boy could help in the fields or the youngest girl could help with domestic tasks. That usually meant three to four years after the last birth. It was the grandparents' responsibility to tell their "ways" of family planning to the young couple.

18. Rondavals, *round mud-and-twig huts, are typical of homes in rural Zambia.*

These traditions were still maintained in the villages, but what happened in the towns? There were no grandparents to talk to the young married couples, who usually were too shy to talk about family planning with others. So they often had a child a year, and these large, unplanned families were too expensive to support on a limited income during a time of high inflation. The children and mothers were not healthy, and large families were placing serious strain on marriages.

Margaret saw an unmet need: young parents needed to be able to *read* the literature on contraceptives.

Kitwe, 1995

Our small plane landed at the tiny airport at Ndola. It was a tense landing, but we had a good pilot.

On we went to Kitwe, where I gave workshops in literacy. While there, I contacted the mining people, for this was the site of some of the biggest copper mines in the world. We were fortunate to get special permission to visit the "townships"—the compounds where the miners and their families lived. We visited nurseries, nutrition classes, welding classes, and agricultural projects. Most interesting to me was the township library. The simple building was plain but adequate, with library tables, chairs, and plenty of bookshelves. But at most, there were fifty books on the shelves. There were rows and rows of *empty* shelves!

Our guide picked out several books, showing the old publication dates and the tattered pages. He explained that paper and books were expensive in Zambia. Here was a real unmet need—books. I saw young men reading back issues of English newspapers, their only up-to-date information, but I also saw on each library table communist booklets, in English. I picked one up, looking questioningly at our guide. "Yes, communist literature," he told me. "They send it to us free. Our young people are hungry for anything to read. You in the United States can, you know, lose the Cold War, but it needn't be so. Just send us books—any kind, technical, history, fiction, even propaganda for the USA."

This was a shock to us. Learning to read is so important that we sometimes forget that reading materials, of any kind, are just as important.

I picked up one of the communist propaganda booklets, asking if I might take it home to show what was being sent out. Our guide readily agreed, and I tucked it inside my suitcase and forgot all about it.

In Johannesburg a few weeks later, we told our friends about the communist literature I had brought into South Africa in my suitcase. They were aghast: "You don't mean you have that in your suitcase right here?"

"Yes, of course I do."

"Do you know that if any communist literature was found in your suitcase here in South Africa, you'd be jailed for at least five years?"

I laughed, thinking they were joking. But they weren't. In fact, they told me that if it was found in my suitcase in *their* house, they, too, would be jailed for five years. They were dead serious, and being a citizen of the United States wouldn't help me at all.

I really didn't want to destroy that pamphlet. They suggested that perhaps I take a picture of it and *then* destroy it. Really, we all felt better after we had burned it.

We sometimes forget there isn't real freedom in many parts of the world, including the freedom to read whatever one wants.

Prison in Zambia

*An earlier version of this article appeared
in the* Syracuse Post-Standard *on January 19, 1996.*

I used Language Experience, through a translator, to break the ice in a tense situation in a maximum security prison in Kabwe, Zambia. The Commissioner of Prisons had told me that 10 percent of the inmates in his charge were literate, 15 percent semiliterate, and 75 percent completely illiterate.

Language Experience is a technique for getting students involved in their own learning—for the teacher to write down the students' words, teaching them to read their own words and in that way become authors.

As I walked into a bare room in the prison in Kabwe, I saw perhaps twenty men dressed in ragged white shorts and tops made of old mealie-meal sacks. They stood with heads down, listening to the instructor talk in Bembe, their language. Soon the instructor indicated that it was my turn to talk. What does one say to tough-looking prisoners who cannot read and write their own language?

I plunged in. Through a translator, I asked what *they* wanted to talk about. No response. It seems that no one had ever asked them what *their* interests or concerns were. Again: "What do you like best to do?" And I pointed to one young man. He looked up in surprise, then said, "ulimi," which means "farming." I had the translator write *ulimi* on the board. I asked the next man: "woodworking," he told me, and we wrote it on the board in Bembe. A third told me, "dancing."

Already they had given me three choices, and I reminded them that Zambia was now a democracy and that in my classes each man had one vote. They could vote for what *they* wanted to talk about: farming, woodworking, or dancing.

Heads came up as they talked among themselves in Bembe. They came alive as they voted by raising their hands. I counted in English, the translator in Bembe; what clapping when *ulimi* won!

I reminded them that they knew more about farming than I did. After that, we could hardly keep up with writing the words that spilled from them. After arguing among themselves, they finally agreed how their story would start: "Ulimi wabwino chifukwa uphasa chakudya," which means "Farming is important to give us food."

I then taught them to read their own words, reminding them that *they* were the authors. Yes, they were sight words, but it was the beginning of teaching syllable sounds, using their words as key words. From *ulimi*, I used the syllable *li* to teach the other syllables *la, le, li, lo, lu*—then the syllable *mi* to teach *ma, me, mi, mo,* and *mu*.

Copying the words they had spoken from the board, they started making their own first reader.

A first step, but an important first step. I wished I could have stayed to continue the lessons. I can only hope a seed was planted and that they have continued with learner-centered lessons.

Zenith Construction Company

After I had spoken to a Rotary meeting in Lusaka, one of the members, Grant Pistor, came to challenge me. He was in charge of a construction company, and most of his men couldn't read or write in the local language, Nyanja. Could I help them?

I offered to work with ten of the men on Saturday mornings. He said he'd invite all thirty-six of his men but assured me that only a few would show up. What a surprise to both of us when twenty-five men appeared for the first class. We gathered in an unfinished

19. Working with construction laborers, I found them anxious to learn to read and write in Nyanga, their language. They sang their thanks to me, their new "Auntie Ruth."

building—rough concrete floor, cement block walls, openings for windows. For benches, they brought their own cement blocks and long pieces of lumber. Mr. Pistor had provided a chalkboard and markers for me.

What do you do and where do you start when you don't know their language? I had requested a translator, who turned out to be one of their group who did know English. What do you do when you have no idea of their reading or writing skills or whether they've been to school at all?

I introduced myself (through the interpreter), suggesting that they call me "Auntie Ruth." Africans are comfortable calling anyone older "auntie" or "uncle." I asked each man to write his name, and because Nyanja is phonically regular, it was easy for me to pronounce each name nearly correctly from the spelling. I went to each one, saying his name, asking how many years he'd been in school. Most had been in school from four to nine years, but three had never attended and couldn't write their names.

Through the interpreter, I asked what they wanted to talk about. I found that all Africans consider their villages their real homes, no matter where they work or raise their families. And they like farming and want to learn more about it. So they talked about farming and their villages, and I wrote down what they said, teaching them their own words. They were excited. In later lessons, I would find that they wanted to know the written words for many of the terms used in construction and that they wanted to write letters to their loved ones.

Singing is important to Africans, who harmonize beautifully. When I suggested that they teach me a song, they laughed and started right in—

> Tiyende pamodzi, Tiyende pamodzi
> Ndimtima umodze, Ndimtima umodze,
> Aunty Ruth tiye, Tiyende pamodzi ndimtima umodze

—entreating me to come work with them. I joined in their singing, swaying to the rhythm, ending each session with fun and laughter.

Bob's Funeral/Prison Project

In Zambia, as in most of Africa, the biggest and most expensive event in one's life is one's own funeral. The family is expected to give a big feast, with meals for a week and relatives coming from far and wide. The debts incurred can take a lifetime to repay.

In talking to a young widow who owned a funeral parlor, Bob learned that when a person dies, his or her body is wrapped in a sheet and a blanket and buried in a rather ostentatious casket. The family must purchase the sheet and blanket and the coffin as well as all the necessary food for family and friends. She told him that the price for an elaborate casket with crude plastic handles had escalated, and that with the other expenses, the family often couldn't pay her. What could she do?

A problem—and Bob is a problem solver. First, why not buy sheets and blankets in bulk and sell them to bereaved families at less than what they would have had to pay? She'd even make a small profit on them.

As for the casket, why not go to the prison? I had told Bob that the prisoners had no jobs. When Zambia was under British rule, many of the men, including prisoners, had been trained as carpenters. Wood was available. Why not contract with the prison to make simple wooden caskets with rope handles? A win–win situation—jobs for the prisoners and cheaper, more practical caskets for the funerals.

But how would she get paid? The families had so little money. Bob had noticed that most rural Zambians made and sold charcoal. They'd pack it in large bags and sell it to truckers, who would come by, pick the bags up, and sell them at a good profit in the city.

Bob had another suggestion: Why not have the families pay the funeral costs in charcoal? Bartering was a new concept to her. Her son, who had an old truck, could take the charcoal and sell it for a profit in the city. Another win–win situation—she would get her money and the families could pay their debts.

We've found that problem solving, creativity, and the willingness to work within the customs of others are all basic to helping others.

Five Polio Victims

This article first appeared in the Syracuse
Post-Standard *on January 12, 1996.*

Five young Zambian men, all crippled victims of polio, were struggling to survive in a crowded area of Lusaka, Zambia. They wouldn't beg. They asked for no charity. They were striving to help themselves.

Bob walked into the cluttered, unkempt, small cement building, the Polio Rehab Center of the University Training Hospital in Lusaka. He was greeted by Chisenga Obete's warm smile. Chisenga's sparkling eyes kept Bob from looking at his wasted legs as he maneuvered his battered wheelchair to come closer and shake hands, African style—a regular handshake, then grabbing the thumb and back to a regular handshake.

Yes, this was the place—Appropriate Paper Technology Enterprises Ltd. Yes, they did make papier-mâché products for sale. Darius Banda moved crablike, throwing his thin leg forward as he rested on the metal brace attached to his arm, pushing his left arm toward Bob. Then Kenneth Habarru, the leader, whose left arm and side were withered, quietly walked up to Bob.

This was not what Bob expected on being assigned by the International Executive Service Corps to a company with the prestigious name of Appropriate Paper Technology Enterprises Ltd.

That first morning together brought the start of friendship and understanding, a new appreciation for a true self-help project.

Paper and cardboard boxes had been donated by embassies and foreign government groups. The men cut them into the desired shapes, adding layer upon layer of flour and water paste, allowing them to dry and harden.

It was surprising how strong yet how lightweight the items were. A small table was their best-selling item, while a large bin to store mealie-meal was the most expensive and difficult to make.

Their customers? Only the few people who happened to come to this remote area of the hospital compound. So their income, after buying flour and paints, was minimal. They had no idea of pricing, thinking only to get back the cost of the material used.

Kenneth kept good records. He totaled all income monthly and all expenses. Whatever was left over was divided among the five men. Bob was shocked when he learned that their average monthly income was 60,000 *kwacha*—about $75—for all five men, giving each approximately 12,000 *kwacha* or $15 a month. How could they live on it? They admitted they often went to bed hungry.

Bob's instinct and desire was to give them the money, but his purpose was to build an ongoing money-making project. How to do it?

First a new name—"Light Weight Products"—with a colorful butterfly as the logo stating, "Light as a butterfly." Then new salable products with Zambian designs. A small nest of tables, jewelry, an African bowl.

They needed an African artist's help. While on the train to Livingston, we had met Kwame Orchere, a well-known Ghanian artist teaching in Lusaka, who agreed to work pro bono with the men on color and design.

What about marketing? Bob scouted around the hospital, convincing the head nurses that there should be a stand where gifts could be purchased for patients. The manager of our hotel shared used hotel drapes for displaying the new gifts. Plans included displaying at hotels and gift shops.

What about pricing? The men hadn't thought that their time had value, real money value. Bob suggested they record the number of hours spent on each article and include that as they considered prices. We looked around at prices of competitive articles for their comparison.

We discouraged the idea of taking out a loan, for the interest in Zambia was from 30 percent to 60 percent. Instead, Bob suggested budgeting, looking forward to a small but growing nest egg to be used for purchasing supplies as well as increased income for the men.

Light Weight Products, with its colorful butterfly logo, was on its way. The men beamed. They could see a light at the end of their tunnel, new hope, renewed faith.

We wanted to know more. "Do you mean you make supports for the polio children here?" They proudly displayed a stand they had made whereby children with polio, whose legs were nearly useless, could grab on and stand erect, sometimes for only a few seconds, building up leg strength over time.

These five men, crippled themselves and living on next to nothing, had looked beyond themselves, working to help those polio children who couldn't help themselves. That's real love. I was reminded again of the familiar biblical passage: "Faith, Hope, and Love, but the greatest of these is Love."

Bags of Money

Bob had gone to one of the banks in Lusaka to close out our account, for we had completed our assignment and were preparing to return home. In front of him in line was a man with two huge suitcases. As they came to the teller, the man opened the suitcases. They were filled with money—$50,000. Because of inflation, each American dollar was worth 800 *kwacha*, the local currency, making 800 times that number of bills. A small machine was used to count the money.

While waiting the hour it took to count the money, Bob got acquainted with the gentleman. He was head of a project for the Seventh-day Adventists. He had gotten word that the bank where they had kept their money was going under, and they wouldn't cash his check. So he had gone back with suitcases, withdrawn the money, and was now depositing it in this bank.

The gentleman was interested to know what we, as Whites, were doing in Zambia. Bob told him we were with the International Executive Service Corps, that he was working to help small businesses, and that I was working on a literacy project. "Literacy? That's just what we need. Can your wife help our headmistress and our teachers?"

Bob explained that we had completed our assignment and were leaving in three days for home. We were sorry, but it was too late to help them.

The next morning, early, there was a knock on the door of our hotel room. I opened it to a White woman I had never seen before, who told me, "I'm Terri Horner, with the Seventh-day Adventists. Our director met your husband yesterday, and he said you taught literacy. I need your help."

I remembered Bob's story of the bank and told her, "I'm sorry, but we're leaving in two days for home. If I had known sooner, I would have been able to help you." She stood there quietly, so I invited her in for a cup of tea.

Terri Horner repeated, "I need your help." She explained that she and her family had been in Zambia for five years and that her husband had died nine months earlier of malaria. Now she was the headmistress of their school, and she tried to describe how she was teaching. It was sad—I could have helped her. But then, why help her when I knew nothing of the work of the Seventh-day Adventists?

I had many last-minute duties, and I was tired after my many weeks in Zambia, but I couldn't resist Terri's request. I agreed to give a condensed three-hour training for her and several of her young Zambian teachers (which I did), on the condition that she show me her projects and what they were doing.

Terri Horner and a driver picked me up, and I spent an entire day with them visiting their farm, school, and villages. Absolutely amazing! About twenty-five years ago the Seventh-day Adventists had purchased three thousand acres of land by a river. The goal was to be self-supporting and to teach and help the Zambians there. They raised maize, bananas, guava, pawpaw, mango, oranges, even gum trees (the straight poles are perfect for buildings). They raised sunflowers, crushing the seeds to make oil for sale. They had a big maize distribution center—people came from faraway villages. Everything grown was sold except for the lemons on the lemon trees—those were *given* to anyone who was sick and were used especially to treat malaria. Everything was clean and well organized: all the buildings were painted (lower half maroon, upper half white), and the grounds were attractive, with about ninety acres under irrigation, the water being piped in from the river.There were about 220 people at the institute—workers and staff, with thirty-three students in the primary school and thirty-three in the nursery school. There were four teachers plus the headmistress.

Instead of playing games at recess, the children raked the paths and grass, which instilled in them a sense of pride in *their* school. The desks were made from their own wood in their own shops, and they even made their own slates (particleboard painted black). They made their own uniforms to give experience to the older girls as well as for income. They had their own curriculum, based on the Bible—English, math, science, social studies, and of course Bible studies. I asked how their school compared with government schools and was told it was hard to compare, but every time one of their students left and went to a government school (no secondary school here yet), he or she was first in the new class.

The local language was Tonga, but the school was run in English. Sometimes it took the youngsters several years to catch on to English. The local teachers who spoke Tonga had no teacher training, and the foreign teachers had no training in how to teach English as a second language.

One young man, Israel, eighteen years old, couldn't read or write in Tonga and couldn't speak, read, or write English. He wanted so badly to learn that he came to the grade-one class. He didn't mind the embarrassment—learning was his motivation.

I noticed that all the teachers were men. They had tried local women and found that most of them didn't have the strength of character to stand up when things got tough. No matter how capable the local women were, when they were up against a man, they folded. In their minds, a man was always superior to a woman. I must admit that in other areas of IESC work—even in management areas—women were most capable when they were with other women. As soon as a man, even a less competent one, came into the picture, the women usually gave in to him. Their saying was "When pants come in . . ."

One never knows when a door is opened. Having helped Terri Horner in Zambia, I was invited to give training at the International Headquarters of the Seventh-day Adventists in Silver Springs, Maryland, which in turn let to invitations to give literacy training in Papua New Guinea, the Solomon Islands, and Cambodia. So it goes—from one open door to another.

 Swaziland, 1988 and 1991–92

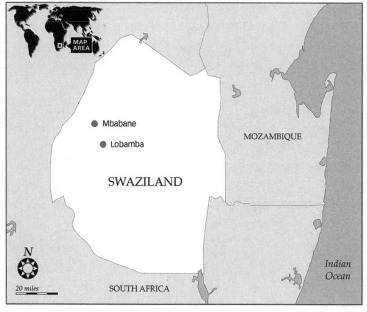

Map of Swaziland by Peter Allen.

We were in a real African kingdom, the Kingdom of Swaziland. His Majesty King Mswati III, the twenty-three-year-old king, and *Indlovukazi* (queen mother) Ntombi, ruled this tiny kingdom in southern Africa.

An earlier version of the material on pages 89–95 appeared in the Syracuse Post-Standard *on April 18, 1992.*

How the King Is Chosen

Swaziland was a British Protectorate until 1968. Much-loved eighty-one-year-old King Sobhuza died in 1982, and a new king, a fourteen-year-old boy, was chosen to succeed him. He was crowned King Mswati III in 1986, when he was eighteen.

Two kinds of marriage are recognized in Swaziland: Western, where a man takes only one wife, and traditional, where a man may take several wives. The king, though, is expected to have many wives and many children, especially sons.

When the king dies, all the men and unmarried women shave their heads. A married woman must shave the base of her head and wear a white woolen cord around it. Members of the Royal Family wear special strings around their waists. Widows are in mourning for two years, wearing black from head to foot. The men wear black bands on their left arms, except for those in the army, who wear black bands on their right arms.

The king never knows who his heir will be. After Sobhuza's death, the Royal Council of the Parliament in Lobamba chose the heir from among the old king's many sons, considering the mode of marriage as well as the background of the wife and the boy's mother. If the country had been at war, the council probably would have chosen an elder son with more experience, but because the country was at peace, a younger son was chosen so that he could be trained carefully in Swazi traditions.

The mother of the son chosen is automatically the next queen mother, who serves as adviser and co-ruler. With this in mind, all of the king's wives strive to get along, for they never know which of them will be the next queen mother. The Royal Family of Swaziland, the Dlaminis, do not intermarry, which means that the king is always a Dlamini, whereas the queen mother is never a Dlamini but someone of another noble family.

The *Ngwenyama* (lion) of Swaziland is not only chief, head of administration, and constitutional monarch, but the embodiment of the entire nation. It is believed that his health reflects the nation's prosperity and that his fertility reflects the fertility of the nation's soil.

My Work in Swaziland

English and siSwati are the official languages of Swaziland. In the urban areas most people understand and speak English; in rural areas only siSwati is spoken. SiSwati has been a written language for only four or five decades, so there is little reading material in siSwati.

The 1988 census had found that the illiteracy rate in Swaziland was 30 percent. In other words, one out of three Swazis could not "read a simple sentence or write their own name" in siSwati. Probably 60 percent could not understand, speak, read, or write English well enough to find jobs or advance in their present jobs. For thirty years, the Sebenta (*sebenta* means *work*) National Institute had been working on literacy at the grassroots level, organizing classes and training "volunteer" instructors, each of whom received a modest honorarium. My work was with the Sebenta National Institute.

Before helping with literacy training in Swaziland, I insisted on visiting the rural areas, to see the literacy classes in the villages. At first, the leaders told me that riding in the truck would be too hard. "No problem," I said. Then they said that because the roads were often impassable, they sometimes had to leave the truck and walk for long distances. I glanced down at my low-heeled shoes and said, "No problem." But the villagers only speak siSwati, they told me. "No problem," I replied. "There are many ways to communicate, and *you* speak siSwati. *You* can be my translators." So we drove to several rural villages where only siSwati was spoken.

Village Women Walking to Class

The roads in Swaziland are rugged—some of them are simply rock-strewn riverbeds—and several times we were forced to leave the car and walk. We saw women working their fields up to the last minute before classes, and we saw them walking to class, babies on

20. *Time is casual in Swaziland, and even lessons cannot be exact. Women walk, then wait for the teacher, chatting and relaxing from their busy lives.*

their backs and books in hand, leaving their work for a few hours of study.

A group of women were sitting and chatting on a hilltop while waiting for their teacher. The teachers often had to travel from other villages. Buses were not always dependable, and the volunteer teachers often had limited funds and couldn't afford the bus fare. The women had learned that even dedicated teachers were often late.

After we became friends, they let me carry a baby, African style, on my back, sharing their friendship. Most of the learners were women—most men were hesitant to admit their lack of basic skills, and many had gone to South Africa to work in the mines.

Teacher in Rural Swaziland

The most important person in any literacy program is the learner, followed closely by the teacher or instructor. Let me introduce you to a rural instructor.

21. Teaching is often done under the trees, with a broken blackboard in place of books.

Nellie Mhlabane was a grandmother with six years of schooling, living in the village of Mgungundlovu. In 1986 she took the Sebenta instructor's training and, as a "volunteer," returned to her village to teach other adults who couldn't read or write in their mother tongue, siSwati. She continued to teach two literacy classes a day, two hours each, with thirteen in one class and eight in the other. Most of her classes were held under a big tree in the village, using a simple chalkboard and large pictures of African life to motivate discussions of "generative" (meaningful) words, which she taught by syllables.

Just a year before our visit, while she was imparting enthusiasm for learning in her village, other mothers decided to build a school for their children. With their chief's support, and with their own hands, they built a three-room school building with cement blocks and plaster walls.

Why Swazi Women Want to Learn to Read

Lindiwe Msisi was in the Sebenta class in the village of Ngabam-blopha. Lindiwe was a "peddler"—that is, a person with a license to sell goods in a limited area of Swaziland. She often went to South Africa to get pots, pans, bed linen, and household goods, which she then sold at a modest profit to local Swazis. Peddlers were often looked down upon, but I always insisted that Lindiwe and other peddlers were entrepreneurs to be admired and respected.

In the past, Lindiwe had been able to get a passport and pass border controls by giving only her "thumb signature." But the rules were getting stricter—the border guards were now insisting that she sign her name. Once Lindiwe could sign her name, she wanted more: she wanted to read and write whatever she needed in siSwati, and she wanted to understand and speak English and eventually read and write it. She would be able to get better goods and better prices in South Africa, and make a better living for herself and her family.

Yes, Swazis knew the importance of learning to read, but with their busy daytime lives, evenings were their only free time. There was no electricity in the rural areas. Some homesteads used kerosene lanterns, but candles, made by hand, were used by most Swazis who wanted those extra hours of study. They knew how important it was to be close to the light, whether that light was their lone candle or the "light of the world," as suggested by their pastor.

In the class with Lindiwe were seven other women. They sat on straw mats inside the dark, thatch-roofed *rondaval* (hut). There was limited reading material in siSwati, and I wanted to get them more involved in making reading materials for themselves. So I asked them to tell me some of the things that were happening in their village. They were hesitant at first. But they talked among themselves—in siSwati, of course–and the teacher translated for me.

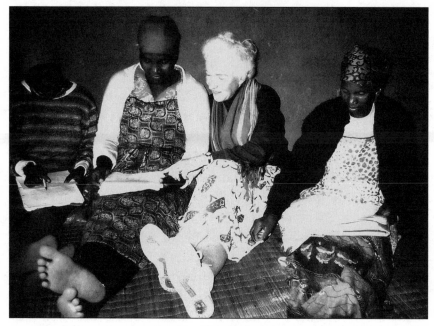

22. *Ruth sitting on a* rondaval *floor with her students, learning together and sharing stories.*

Many of the children in the village had been sick all month, and two had died, so many of the mothers, including those in the class had had to stop their peddling temporarily. It made them more determined than ever to learn reading and writing, so that they could help their children in the schooling they were missing, as well as write their names on government documents, keep the records they now must keep, and help themselves read the government health pamphlets.

I was excited—here was a wonderful story. We wrote their words in siSwati on the chalkboard, teaching them their own words. They, too, were excited, but several of them told me that their eyes watered even after a short time of reading. I realized how dark in was in the *rondeval,* which had only slits for windows. I asked about kerosene lanterns, or candles. Too expensive to use every day, they told me. Their eyes hurt, they said.

I realized that *I* was wearing my reading glasses. Did they need reading glasses, too? I took my glasses off and handed them to the first woman. Gently she put them on, and her happy grin told the story—she could see better. One by one, each of the seven women tried them on, laughing when they found they could see better. The last woman handed my glasses back. Oh, how I wanted to leave the glasses, but they were the only ones I had with me. But now I knew one way I could help.

Back in Mbabane, I told Bob, "I know what I want for Christmas."

Being far from home, he was pleased to know that he could do something special for me for Christmas.

"I want four pairs of reading glasses," I told him.

He looked surprised, but as he listened to my story, he agreed. And my four pairs of reading glasses for Christmas went to my siSwati class in Ngabamblopha.

• • •

Native-Language Books in siSwati

Back in Mbabane, I visited the children's section of their lovely library. There were stacks of children's books, but all in English. Where were the children's books in siSwati? There were fewer than a dozen. Well, perhaps there would be more in the adult section. But no—there were only eight books in siSwati there.

Sebenta had some books in siSwati, but they were available only to its students. I learned there was a daily siSwati newspaper. The owner told me it was just holding its own but that it was circulated in the villages. As well, the New Testament had been translated into siSwati, and learning to read the Bible was a high priority of many villages.

A Woman Entrepreneur in Swaziland

Norma Khohze had been assigned the task of taking care of us in Swaziland, where we worked as volunteer executives for the IESC. She cooked, cleaned, did the laundry, and generally made life easier for us. But Norma had another life—she was a peddler (or hawker). As mentioned earlier, a peddler bought and sold goods and needed a license to sell in a specified area.

Norma's husband had left her and her four children—one of whom was mentally handicapped—and had gone to Johannesburg, South Africa, for a freer life. She had tried to get him to help support his family, but he had refused, and there was no means for her to insist. Whenever she could, she got temporary jobs as a domestic or maid. She needed more money, but she had no other salable skills.

So Norma did what many Swazi women do—she applied for a peddler's license. That was in 1978, and she had learned much as a small business owner, for that is exactly what she was.

Norma traveled by bus once a month to Johannesburg, where she had located wholesalers. She bought pots and pans, linens, and clothes, and sold them to friends and old customers. They had to place a deposit of 50 percent if they ordered goods in advance. The more credit they asked for, the higher the price.

She stayed overnight on the bus and returned with all her wares, often several huge bundles. There was no charge for this baggage as long as each bundle was small enough that the bus driver could throw it onto the roof of the bus.

Norma kept her money under her blouse, slipping it in through the collar. Only once had she been robbed, in Durban. The thieves worked in gangs—while one man got her attention, another reached right in and grabbed the money. They had been watching her, noting that she had money and where she kept it. They often slapped a tiny sign on a peddler's back, signaling the other gang members whom to target. Luckily for her, she had already made her purchases, so all they got was the money she'd saved for the 10 percent customs duties. How did she pay the border fee? Someone on the bus loaned her the money. The peddlers watched out for one another.

Peddling had given Norma a good living, for she had built a steady clientele. Competition was fierce, so she had learned to keep track of her costs—not just the prices she paid for goods but also the travel and time costs, the bad-debt costs, and her profit margin.

The women of Swaziland were good businesswomen, whether they were traveling peddlers or worked from market stalls. These hard-working women were the backbone of small business in Swaziland as well as the support for their families.

How I Got Permission to Take Pictures of Incwala

Incwala is the big traditional celebration where the Swazis celebrate the first fruits of their labor and the end of the Swazi year.

Invitations to observe the last day of the Big Incwala are extended to a handful of diplomats and ambassadors, who sit in a special area. However, they are not allowed to take photos. Even so, I applied to attend and take photographs and was told at the time that I was unlikely to get a permit.

Then someone called from the broadcasting station and told me that I needed to come down and discuss my application. I met Zakes Nkambule, who was very severe, telling me that Swazis at Incwala don't want photos taken of them. Their customs are strict, and when a permit is given, it is to someone who has attended Incwala in the past and who knows what is permissible. So it would be impossible for me to attend, never mind take pictures. I accepted his ruling, but then I told him of our work at Sebenta.

Mr. Nkambule told me that he had been a teacher before becoming a broadcaster. I told him about my dreams of peace, about helping people know and understand one another's cultures and traditions, and that I wanted to share with America what I had learned about the Swazis. We talked for nearly two hours.

Mr. Nkambule was especially proud of one daughter, Lettie, who was the secretary to the Swazi ambassador to the United States. That gave me an idea. Because Bob and I had a son in Washington, DC, and would be seeing him on our return home, I suggested that I take his picture and take it to her as a surprise from her father. And while I was in Washington with her, I'd take her picture and send it to him. He was delighted. And then he arranged for me to have one of the few permits to take limited pictures at Incwala.

The Little Incwala

The full ceremony of Incwala includes the Little Incwala and ceremonial dances in the villages, and lasts over a week.

On the night of the full moon in December or January, a regiment of pure young boys, twelve to eighteen or twenty years old, marches to Enhlambeni, twenty miles into the countryside, singing traditional songs. They cut branches from the sacred acacia trees, which will be used for the king's shelter, the *lusekwana*. Some of the boys wear traditional costumes, others are in street clothes or Boy Scout shirts.

The boys are led by men in traditional costumes: feathers, leopard skins, and cattle-tail cloaks. Some carry drums or trumpets. They are divided into regiments according to age. Clan loyalties are strong in Swaziland, but regimental ties are just as strong, uniting the country's many clans.

Each *lusekwane* boy carries a large cutting from the sacred grove. After the king enters the King's Kraal, the site of the celebration, they march in slowly, in rhythm to their singing, to deliver the branches for the king's secret ritual. Only a few boys are selected for the ceremony of catching a special black bull. We've heard two accounts of that ceremony: one says that the boys kill the bull with their bare hands, the other that the boys catch the bull and make it lie down so that the king can mount it to perform whatever ritual is necessary.

The Little Incwala lasts two days, starting when the sun reaches its southern solstice and the moon is dark.

The Big Incwala

An earlier version of this article appeared
in the Syracuse Post-Standard *on May 9, 1992.*

The Big Incwala lasts six days, beginning on the night of the full moon. Many secret rituals are performed by and on the king during Incwala, so that by the last day everything is purified. We had been invited to witness the final great celebration.

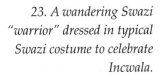

23. A wandering Swazi "warrior" dressed in typical Swazi costume to celebrate Incwala.

The King's Kraal was enclosed by thousands of saplings bound together to form a dense fence twelve feet high. Thousands of Swazis were milling about, all in traditional dress.

A fierce-looking Swazi warrior shuffled alone into the open field of the King's Kraal in Lobamba, the traditional capital of Swaziland. He wore an ancient leopard-skin loincloth and dusty cow tails as a shawl, holding his cowhide shield and stick proudly, walking barefoot. As we got closer, we could see why he lagged behind the thousands of Swazi warriors rushing to enter the king's byre—he was old and frail, though his back remained straight.

He turned and looked around, saw someone, and beckoned to that person to follow him. A small boy ran up to him, wearing a miniature version of his grandfather's dress. He stretched his short legs as he tried to follow, step by step, holding his own small stick high. Together, grandfather and grandson followed the younger Swazi warriors toward the high fence.

I displayed my photographer's permit, then I followed the pair through a gap in the fence to get my first view of the spectacular sight.

The king's cattle byre was filling up with thousands of shouting, whistling Swazi men wearing leopard skins and cow-tail shawls and carrying shields and sticks, running to enclose the huge circular byre.

From the opposite end of the byre came the hundreds of women of the royal family, the queens as well as the king's sisters, daughters, and wives. All were barefoot and wore ankle-length black skirts. Most wore a *mahiya*, the black, white, and red (or orange) traditional Swazi cloth over one shoulder, leaving one arm bare. Others wore individualized colorful cloths, and one beautiful young woman, a princess, wore a maroon silk *mahiya* dotted with gold medallions. I learned that she worked for an insurance company in London—one never knows the occupations of those who observe Incwala. Some will be lawyers or members of Parliament, others will be mechanics or teachers, still others clan elders or chiefs from the rural areas.

You knew that most of the women were married for they had tied white string around their short black hair at the hairline to signify marriage. And those of the king's family had stuck red feathers in their hair. Because this is a polygamous culture, there were many royal princesses.

As we watched the women slowly dancing and chanting, I noticed young girls gathering. Breasts bared, they wore multicolored beaded miniskirts, swaying in time with the soft chanting. Gradually the women made a circle, enclosing the young dancing girls.

A trumpet sounded, and all faces turned to a gap in the fence next to the small, covered review stand, where the dignitaries were sitting with their wives. Entering the byre through the gap were a dozen older, heavyset men wearing elegant black-and-white feathered headdresses above their leopard skins and cow-tail shawls. They were followed by His Majesty Mswati III, wearing his own feathered headdress and traditional costume. The tall, slender king had been in seclusion for days, following the traditional but secret rituals prescribed by his mother and the elders. Accompanying him was a young boy, whose presence signified the importance of passing along the Swazi traditions.

This day of joy was the culmination of Incwala. All were invited to join in the slow, rhythmic dance. I, too, joined in, and the Swazis clapped, pleased that I was enjoying Incwala with them.

Our Sebenta Guard as We Return "Home"

When we returned to our home at Sebenta at dusk, the gates were locked. I jumped out of the car, calling to the guard that we were home. "Hello . . . ?" No answer. "Hello . . . ?" A voice from above answered "Hello!" I looked around—no one was there.

Then I looked up. There was our guard in the tree. We both laughed as I snapped his picture. That was very clever of him. He could watch Sebenta without anyone seeing him, and I'm sure he could take a little snooze, too.

A Chinese Proverb on the Wall of a Swazi School

Go to the people, live among them, love them.
Start with what they know,
Build on what they have,
But of the best leaders,
When their task is accomplished,
Their work done, the people all remark:
  "We have done it ourselves."

We were surprised to learn that a nationally known agency had been called in to help them the year before we were there. The Sebenta people were highly dissatisfied. Why? I read the agency's report—it was outstanding in that it described all the problems. What they didn't do was give suggestions of where the Swazis could help themselves. We made suggestions, but the Swazis had to do it themselves. They did, for the following year they won the International Reading Association's $10,000 prize for the most improved literacy project.

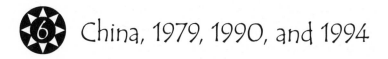

✦⁶ China, 1979, 1990, and 1994

RUSSIA

MAP AREA

MONGOLIA

Harbin

NORTH KOREA

Beijing

Sea of Japan

SOUTH KOREA

CHINA

JAPAN

East China Sea

Disputed territory

INDIA

Gweilin

Fuzhou

MeiZhou

TAIWAN

N

Nanning

MYANMAR

VIETNAM

Hong Kong

LAOS

THAILAND

200 miles

Map of China by Peter Allen.

Did you ever, as a child, dig a hole, thinking, "If I dig deep enough, I'll get to China?" And what if someone in China was digging, too—would you meet them halfway? What would you have found in China in 1979? We found more than nine hundred million people, most of them wearing identical outfits—navy baggy pants, navy tops, and straw peasant hats or Mao caps. They were trying so hard to be equal that they even dressed alike.

What language is spoken by most people in the world? Mandarin, the official language of China. What is number two? English. But in 1979, many of the billion people in China wanted English as a second language. More and more Chinese were realizing that English is the major language of business and world communication.

In the following decades, China would open itself to joint ventures (business arrangements between Chinese and foreigners, especially the United States and Canada), and facility with English would open up new job opportunities. Thus, by the time of our first visit, the demand was already rising for English instruction.

China has often been called a "sleeping giant," and in the late 1970s this sleeping giant was awakening. Demand for consumer goods—televisions, refrigerators, washing machines, and even microwave ovens—would soon be soaring.

There was a desperate need for better roads, improved agricultural methods, and improved education. There was building and construction everywhere. The Chinese were looking to America as well as to Canada and Japan for technical help. China's billion people were a tempting market for Western goods and would soon be competing strongly with the West as manufacturers.

Communication and understanding between the United States and the People's Republic of China will be imperative if we want peace. China wants to know more about America. Let us in America learn more about China.

What Did We Find in 1979 in China?

We didn't dig a hole, but we flew halfway around the world to Hong Kong and then took the train to Shum Chun, where we saw the first of many huge signs with large Chinese characters. Some had been translated into English:

Long live the great unity of the people of the world.

And:

Unite, strive to build a strong modernized socialist country.

And always there were pictures of former chairman Mao and the then chairman, Hua. Another Chinese slogan was "Punctuality is a virtue," and we soon learned that everything there ran on time, be it a train, an airplane, or your group's bus.

Immediately we saw contrasts. We had left behind the modern skyscrapers of Hong Kong; they had been replaced by water-covered rice paddies and terraced farms and men and women toiling in the fields without machinery. Blue uniforms were everywhere, along with thousands and thousands of bicycles. The few cars were owned by the government; the bicycles were owned by individual Chinese (and were usually their biggest investment). There was even a traffic cop to direct bicycle traffic. Men and women alike carried heavy loads on poles over their shoulders, or they pulled small carts stacked high.

This was our first experience of people staring at us—not a few, but often as many as one hundred. They weren't being rude—just curious, like children looking at a new toy. Through my zoom lens, I could see individual faces and expressions. It was surprising to have a crowd of Chinese watching *us* watching *them*.

24. *In 1979, few Chinese people had seen Westerners. They were curious, not rude, but it was our first experience of people staring at us.*

Suddenly *we* were the minority. We couldn't read the signs. We couldn't understand or speak the language. We couldn't read directions.

What Is a Commune?

The Jenko People's Commune had been founded in 1958. Communes were not a new concept in China—they had been formed from villages that already existed. They were merely a new way of governing. The land was no longer owned by individual landlords—it was owned by all the people in the commune.

The Jenko commune consisted of seventy-five "natural" villages and 120 square kilometers and was home to seventy-five thousand people. Its "mayor" was Liano Thiung Hung, who was in his late forties and lived with his mother, his wife, and their four children. He told me: "Happiness to a Chinese is to be born, live, and die in the same place." When I asked whether people were free to leave the commune, he told me that people were assigned to jobs and communes by the government but that their personal wishes were always considered.

This was an agricultural area. They grew rice, vegetables, and sugar cane and raised livestock. The average income was about $170 per year. There was a cooperative banking system. Yes, more work did provide more pay. What about inflation? Prices were stable, for they were fixed by the government. Houses were individually owned, but not the land, which was owned by the commune. Individuals could have small plots for personal use, and about 20 percent of their income was from this private source.

During the Cultural Revolution, the government attempted to make everyone equal by sending scholars and university students to work in China's rural areas. The people had temporarily lost their respect for scholars and the written word. Several of our guides had been sent to farms to work. They told us it had been difficult for them to return to their studies.

But by 1979, there had been a resurgence in respect for learning. Education for children was compulsory up to the eighth grade. There was a real hunger for knowledge in China. When I asked

25. Education has a high priority in the Chinese culture, and even though books and newspapers weren't available, people stood reading the wall newspapers.

about school discipline, they seemed not to understand my question, which made me wonder whether the problem existed. When I asked how they handled slower students or those with learning problems, our guide told us it was the Chinese way for the better students to help the slower ones—no problem.

Health Problems—and I Have Acupuncture

Chinese clinics and hospitals were primitive by our standards, with medical services costing twenty cents per person per month. Even in 1979, China probably had one of the best medical delivery systems of any developing country. There were three levels of medical services: *preventative*, where each commune had its own first aid people; *brigade*, which included the barefoot doctors who worked among the people; and *clinic*, which included both clinics in local communes and larger hospitals in the cities.

We were hoping to see the Chinese administer acupuncture, but alas, there were no patients the day we visited the commune's

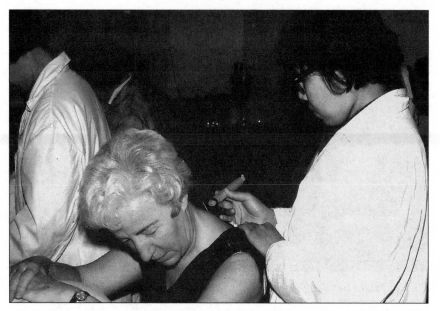

26. *In those early days, acupuncture was not accepted in the United States, and Ruth was determined to try it and learn some of the Chinese ways of healing.*

clinic. So I volunteered. I'd had some pain in my neck and was constantly looking for help. The local doctor found the spots he wanted in my neck and inserted two needles. Then he attached the needles by wires to a primitive battery. Wow—I felt its vibration. Yes, it did help temporarily.

Later, in a hospital in Nanning, I had acupuncture again, this time with better clinical procedures. Again two needles. But this time they were heated by a cigar-shaped lighted object, and the heat pleasantly penetrated down the needles and deep into my neck.

The Institute of Foreign Languages: Zhang Zailiang

In Beijing, I was invited to visit the Institute of Foreign Languages. I had an appointment with Zhang Zailiang, vice chairman of the English Department. Beijing that day had had six inches of snow—the biggest snowfall in years. There were no snowplows, so bicycle and bus traffic was snarled, with people trying to remove

27. Dr. Zhang Zailiang, of the prestigious Institute of Foreign Languages, had invited my taxi driver to join us for lunch; that is "the Chinese way."

the snow with brooms and shovels. My taxi driver spoke only Chinese, and I couldn't understand or speak Chinese, so we couldn't communicate. And because I couldn't read or write in Chinese, I couldn't read any signs or directions.

First we went to the wrong university, then we got stuck in the snow, and finally we arrived at the institute an hour late. There was Zhang Zailiang, waiting for me in the snow. His warm welcome overcame my embarrassment and apologies. He invited me to the austere faculty room for lunch with a senior staff member. Both of them spoke excellent English.

As we started our Chinese meal, Zhang Zailiang asked where my taxi driver was. I told him he was waiting outside to take me back to the hotel—I knew there would be no taxis out here. Zhang politely excused himself, returning a little later with my driver. Zhang knew there was no place for him to eat and had invited him to join us at our table with the faculty.

I got to thinking: How many Americans would be concerned about their taxi driver's lunch and invite him to join them in the faculty room of a prestigious university? In atheist communist China,

Zhang Zailiang was showing by his actions that he lived the country's motto: "Serve the People."

We Americans have much to learn! We need to educate ourselves about other cultures and customs and realize that Americans have no monopoly on helping others.

Kweilin (now Guilin)

Kweilin is a picturesque city in southern China, two thousand years old. This area has long been the inspiration for Chinese painters of traditional landscapes—what we think of as typical Chinese art: tall, round-topped mountains and mist-covered lakes. The people live simply, using every available scrap of land to grow food.

Kweilin was also famous for its magnificent caves. Our Friendship Tour group, many of whom were retired teachers, were visiting the famous Seven Star Caves. To get to that particular site, we had to climb higher and higher. Most of us were huffing and puffing, and many of the elderly teachers found it very difficult and wanted to return. Our guide encouraged them to go on, telling them that the spectacular caves were just ahead. He turned to us and suggested that we "help and love one other—that is the Chinese way."

The younger members of the group and those of us with sturdier legs looked at each other in embarrassment, then went to individual elderly travelers who were having trouble, offering an arm. Together we made our way up to the caves.

The experience reminded me that we Americans don't always practice our beliefs in our daily lives. As I've noted, the motto of atheist China is "Serve the People." We found so many examples of that motto being practiced.

Street Scenes

"Waste not, want not"—"Keep clean"—old American sayings? Well, they're Chinese sayings, too. The streets were always clean, even with the many horses. Looking closely, I saw a little catcher under each horse's tail. The bags caught the droppings, which kept the streets clean, and then the droppings were used as fertilizer. At dusk, young men collected human excrement, running through the streets with "honey buckets" and carrying them to nearby farms.

We often saw men, and women too, sitting on doorsteps, eating their rice from bowls. In China, "rice bowl" is the vernacular for "job." "Breaking a man's rice bowl" means taking away his living. And everyone works—no laziness here.

Kweilin: Number 3 Middle School

Bob and I had seen schools at the commune, and I had visited the Academy of Nationalities, but we wanted to visit a school that was not on the tour. How could we do that?

In Kweilin, we wandered through the maze of side streets. As we entered more unfamiliar areas, we continued our search for schools. Bob carried balloons and a Frisbee—which are wonderful ice breakers—and I carried family photographs to show that we, too, were family people, that we had children and grandchildren.

People were curious and friendly, and we constantly repeated the English word *school*. Sometimes, someone in the crowds that always gathered to look at us spoke a few words of English, and we got general directions by their pointing. Finally, we got two giggling teenagers to write down (in Chinese, of course) the name and address of their school. We showed the paper with the Chinese address as we walked along, and people directed us.

Kweilin Number 3 Middle School was an old school with more than two thousand students. As we entered the compound, we found little boys playing table tennis across an old board, using stones for the net and crude paddles. But they were good, putting a cut on the ball and smashing when the opportunity was there.

As we walked on toward what we thought was the main building, we continued repeating, "English? English?" Finally we located four English teachers.

They were astonished to see us—we were the first foreigners who had ever visited their school. With their limited English, and using gestures, we found that they were trying to teach English but felt very inadequate. Would we help them? We were invited back that night to meet others and talk more.

Luckily, Bob's sense of direction is excellent. He found our way back to our hotel, and he also remembered how to return to the school that night. The city streets weren't lit, and hundreds of black bicycles whizzed by us, their riders wearing dark pants and jackets. We only knew they were there by the bike bells they rang. We learned, too, to trust our noses. When you smelled the pungent odors of latrines, you moved to the side of the road, for it meant that men were coming through carrying "honey buckets" at the ends of long bamboo poles.

We found our way to Kweilin Number 3 Middle School, where the English teachers were waiting for us. They led us into a small classroom, which was crowded with people who were all staring, curious but friendly. Everyone bowed to us, and we returned their bows. Then they offered us tea, heating the water over coals on an ancient black stove in the center of the room. The aroma of unknown herbs greeted our noses while the tea brewed. Over tea, we began to talk.

They had their only tape recorder on the table, an old reel-to-reel type. We dutifully admired it. Then, hesitantly, they asked, because they liked my voice and could understand me, would I please record two or three exercises from their English textbook? Of course. And three hours later, I had taped all the exercises in three complete English books.

Reading their English books opened windows to me. I had been expecting socialist and communist doctrines that told of the virtues of sharing and communal living, so it surprised me that so much of the content had to do with guns, soldiers, and war. It told of Chinese heroes, especially Chairman Mao, but then there came a name—an American or English name—that I did not recognize: Dr. Norman Bethune. I stopped and sipped my tea. Who was Dr. Bethune?

The Chinese in the room were shocked that I, an American, had never heard of Dr. Bethune. But they explained. Dr. Bethune was a Canadian doctor who had joined in the Long March with the Chinese, helping those who needed medical aid. He was one of their great heroes.

When I returned to the United States, I was determined to learn more about Dr. Bethune. I went to our local library, trying to learn more about his life. There was no mention of him anywhere. It couldn't be, could it, that because he sympathized with the Chinese communists, he had been completely left out of American literature? (I later learned that Dr. Bethune was also a national hero in Canada.) That was in 1979. As America strives for truth and knowledge, I hope Dr. Bethune and other Chinese communist heroes will be described in our world history books.

I corresponded later with one of the English teachers I had met, who wrote to me that they were using the tapes I had made in their conversational English classes and that they had made duplicates for use throughout the province. I find it a bit overwhelming that one evening of sharing could touch so many lives.

Nanning: Writer, Editor, Waiter, Teacher?

We were surprised that our visit to Nanning, in southern China just ninety miles from the Vietnamese border, hadn't been canceled. We had arrived the night before fighting began between the Chinese and Vietnamese. We saw troop movements and could sense the tension on the streets.

Nanning at the time was a poor and overcrowded industrial city. Our hotel was modern on the outside but very austere and functional inside.

One young man, wearing a white waiter's jacket and helping at our table, had somehow learned that I was a teacher of conversational English. He was from Harbin University in northern China, where he was an editor and writer, and had been working with twenty colleagues on an English textbook for foundry workers. He told me he was teaching English to the staff of this new hotel. He asked if I'd talk to his English class.

I was confused. He was an editor and writer? And an English teacher? And the waiter at our table? Was this a second or third job?

"Oh, that's the Chinese way," he explained. "Nanning is just recently open to tourists, and few here can speak English." He had volunteered to teach them at night. But why a waiter? He explained that while they were learning, they needed to keep working, so he had volunteered to help them by translating at meal times.

That was very logical Chinese thinking: people needed help, and he was able to help them, so he did. He told me he was following the Chinese motto—"Serve the People."

The Chinese I talked with were amazed when I told them that serving the people was an American tradition, too. The early settlers had depended on one another for help when a barn burned down, or a baby was born, or there was a drought or a flood. People helped each other every day in America. I described to them many of our modern-day programs where Americans continue to help Americans—for example, the thousands of volunteers who teach basic reading and English as a Second Language in my own program, Literacy Volunteers of America.

Nanning: An Apartment Visit

While in Nanning, I gave a demonstration class, teaching conversational English to the staff of our hotel.

We were flattered when the leader of this class invited us to join some of his friends in his home. He lived in a small, bare room in an old apartment building, where nine of us gathered, the others being students from the local university who were studying English. After tea, they asked questions about America and we asked questions about their life in China.

They were *so* pleased with their government's new open policy—that they were free to talk to foreigners without fear of criticism or reprisal. They had been told that America was bad and that imperialist and capitalist countries like the United States did horrible things. They admitted that they really had no knowledge of the United States because they had few books about us and radio news was controlled. They were pleased that the "Gang of Four" was no longer in power, and they realized that they had been wrong about America. They said it must be a great country. They wanted to become America's friends and learn more about our history, our country, and our people.

They asked if I had known any Chinese people. I thought for a minute and remembered my first experience with Chinese. I had had a Chinese Girl Scout troop in Seattle, Washington, when we were first married, back in 1940. I'll never forget that first party I had the girls give for their mothers. I had been astonished to find their mothers arriving in traditional Chinese dress and unable to speak English. The mothers would put their hands together and with great dignity bow to me.

One student spoke up: "They probably were Buddhists, if they put their hands together and bowed."

That was in 1979, and we had been cautioned not to discuss religion or politics. And I had adhered to that policy, but this opening had come from them.

"Are there any Buddhists in China now?" I asked.

They looked at each other, and one student said: "Probably there are some old people who practice their religion in private. They'd be ashamed to do it in public."

"This is Sunday," I replied. "Because we're Christians, we usually go to church on Sunday. Are there any churches near here?"

They became a bit agitated and looked to one another, speaking together in Chinese. Finally the leader said: "No, I don't know of any churches, and I don't know any Christians. But there was a church here in Nanning. It was on the very site where your hotel stands now. It was destroyed during the Cultural Revolution."

The students talked among themselves in Chinese, and finally one of them told me that a priest lived across the hall from this very room. I asked if I could talk with him, but when they went to get him, they found that he was asleep, and they hesitated to wake him. I learned that he was the "cadre" of the building. They explained that in the communist system, each building has a leader called a cadre. It didn't seem unusual to them that a priest would be a cadre. I was told that "anyone who really serves the people can be a cadre."

When we parted, all the students walked us back to our hotel. Each said good-bye and wished us well, thanking us profusely for talking to them. Then one of the quieter students took my hand and said softly, "God bless you."

The year 1979 was a time of transition in China. It still took courage for that quiet Chinese student to say to an American, "God bless you." It told me that America and China could be friends and learn from each other. If we in America come to China with open minds and open hearts, China will certainly respond.

Harbin, 1990: I Am Praised as a "Hen"

Bob and I were invited to a university in Harbin, northern China, for three months in 1990, where I gave training in teaching conversational English to Chinese English teachers.

Professor C, head of the university's English Department, had wanted me to come to China, not to teach a class but to train teachers. The university's president couldn't understand why three months of Literacy Volunteers of America ESL teacher training might be better for China than a year teaching a class.

Professor C put it this way. He reminded Dr. Y of the Chinese saying, "It is good for all Chinese to have an egg-laying hen." Then he added: "Mrs. Colvin is a good egg-laying hen. She's laid hundreds of 'eggs' in the United States, and these eggs have hatched, producing hundreds of groups or affiliates who in turn are laying eggs, producing thousands of volunteer teachers. Wouldn't it be wonderful if she could lay some of her Literacy Volunteer 'eggs' in China, right here in Harbin?"

Icy Blasts of Siberian Snow and Ice

First published by the Syracuse Post-Standard *on March 19, 1990.*

Northern China in the wintertime, with the icy blasts of snow and ice coming down from Siberia! Sounds like the beginning of a novel of the eighteenth century, but that's what northern China was like in the winter of 1990.

Harbin, the city of the ice sculptures, is home to over four million of the more than one billion people in China. It's an industrial city and it's cold.

Our thermometer said five below, and that's not considering the wind factor. So Bob and I donned our long underwear, bottoms and tops; wool slacks and quilted overpants; and two sweaters topped with quilted jackets. Layering—that's the key to keeping warm, for there was a saying in Harbin for the coldest days, "If you can bend over, you haven't enough layers."

We pulled caps over our ears and scarves up over our chins, put on leather wool-lined mittens, wool socks, and insulated boots. The crunching of the snow and the howl of the wind made us realize we were just south of Siberia, and its legendary winters extended to northern China.

Because most transportation in Harbin was by foot, by bicycle, or by bus, a trip to the city meant being prepared to face the cold all day long. It was common to see men in dark quilted coats with fur or quilted hats with huge ear flaps tied under the chin, and children

28. *Ruth and Bob bundled up, layering until they could hardly bend over, to keep warm in this frigid country.*

wearing facemasks. And farmers brought produce, covered by quilted blankets to keep from freezing, on tiny antiquated wooden carts pulled by their small but sturdy shaggy horses.

There were lots of trees. Many streets were lined with trees, barren and bleak at this time of the year, but spring should welcome their budding and leafing.

Outside of the three Americans, one Canadian, three Japanese, and two Russians who too were "foreign experts" at the university, we had seen no foreigners. People stared at us, but a smile and a greeting, *ni hao*, usually got a nod and a smile in return.

In order to get foreign resident permits, we had to have our blood tested. China was doing all it could to prevent AIDS and venereal diseases in the country and insisted that all foreigners who intended to stay for more than a few weeks be tested. We were very hesitant to give blood samples in northern China, for we had heard of their primitive facilities. But we had no choice if we wanted to stay in Harbin for three months.

You enter all public buildings through a door but then must push aside the dark green quilted pads hanging from the ceilings. These pads do help keep the cold out, but they also make the dingy halls very dark, and to us somewhat forbidding. We climbed the four flights of stairs (no elevators here) to room 412, where we gave the appropriate papers, with our passports, to the attendant.

All the attendants in this clinic wore gray-white uniforms, so we weren't sure who was a doctor, who was a nurse, or who was a clerk. One man in a similar uniform was sitting at a desk busily repairing the wiring for a battered tea kettle. It didn't give us much confidence.

Because we spoke no Chinese, we had to depend on gestures. The young lady attendant returned our papers with the official seal and pointed to the stairs up and wrote down the number "520". So—up another flight of stairs.

I felt we were in more of a medical facility in room 520, for there were rows of bottles stacked on the counter by the window. As we waited our turn, I looked around: a mop and a short, crude broom stood by a stained yellow plastic bucket in a corner; a tilted lamp and an electric fan waited for the warm summer weather.

Beyond the glassed-in area, a middle-aged, gray-white-clad female attendant was taking blood from a young Chinese man's arm. A second attendant, a tall Chinese man in the clinic attire, was looking at a blood specimen through a simple microscope, the type we used in high school.

It was my turn next, and my main concern was how I could be sure the needle was sterilized. I sat down, pulled up the sleeves of my sweaters and long underwear. The attendant tied rubber tubing around my arm to better find the vein. She turned aside and reached for the syringe and needle. My sigh of relief may have been audible, for I saw her tear the plastic wrapping off the disposable needle. I felt safe again.

The Chinese attendant was very efficient. I hardly felt her prick my arm and draw blood.

Two days later we received our "red books" certifying that we now were "legal," having our Chinese residents permits.

There are many foreign visitors and guests in the United States. Our experiences as foreign guests in China, not knowing the language or customs, have helped us to understand some of the problems and concerns of those foreign guests living in the United States. I hope we Americans are as helpful and considerate of our foreign guests as they were in Harbin to us.

贰 肆 陆 叁 玖 贰 转 柒 零 柒

29. Chinese characters for a phone number.

First published in the Syracuse Post-Standard *on March 29, 1990.*

When you're in Harbin, China, and a message like the one pictured (fig. 29) is slipped under your door, what do you do?

I showed it to the attendant, who spoke no English. She read the characters silently, made a gesture as using a telephone and wrote down these numbers: 2-4-6-3-9-2-X-7-0-7.

I was delighted and quite smug that I had found out what the message said. I dialed 246-392, smiling at my ingenuity as the phone rang.

A Chinese voice answered. I said, "Extension 707 please." Chinese words. "Seven zero seven." More Chinese words. No communication. I had to say the numbers in Chinese, and I didn't know Chinese.

"Xia xia" (pronounced "she she," meaning "thank you"), and I put the phone down.

Looking in the Chinese-English bilingual dictionary, I learned to say "qi [pronounced *chee* meaning "seven"] ling [meaning "zero"], qi."

I dialed again, got the Chinese operator and said, "Qi, ling, qi." And miracle of miracles, I got my English-speaking Chinese friend.

That taught me the importance of learning Chinese words for numbers.

And little things, like licking an envelope to seal a letter, or licking a stamp to stick it on a letter—not in Harbin, China.

A bottle of milky-looking substance on my desk was the necessary glue. You pour a glob on the envelope or stamp and rub it around with your finger to get the required consistency for sticking. A bit messy, but it worked.

And what about laundry? Most Chinese do their own washing by hand in whatever facilities are available. But here at the university there was a small Japanese washing machine, set on bricks to make it high enough for Westerners. I studied the dials and the machine, and I learned that the left tub was for washing and the tiny right tub had a spin wringer, much like the early Easy Washer made in Syracuse, New York, years ago.

There were two faucets (hot and cold water) over a nearby sink, and a single red tube. You put the clothes in the left tub, attached the tube to the hot-water faucet, putting the other end in the wash tub, and turned on the hot water. When the tub was as full as you thought necessary, you turned off the hot water, removed the tube from the wash tub and turned the wash dial, starting a noisy agitator.

As in the old Easy Washer days, you lifted the clothes to the wringer, drained the water from the wash tub, spun the clothes, returned them to the wash tub by hand for a rinse, and spun dry again. A wire in our bathroom became a clothesline, and the wash was done.

I hadn't used a laundromat for years and forgot that there's usually a long wait. A good book would have helped to pass the time, but there was no bench or chair in this closet-size washroom.

I was warned that there were limited hours for hot water—7 to 9 a.m., noon to 2 p.m., and 7 to 9 p.m. No problem, until one morning when I tried to do my laundry at 8:30, I found no hot water. The hot water first came as a dribble from the hot-water faucet and then stopped. I turned the handle again and again. What was the matter? I still had a half hour of hot-water time.

Evidently there was only so much hot water available, and "the early bird gets the worm." The hot water for Monday morning was used up early. I had to wait until noon to do my laundry.

Yes, we Americans take so much for granted. We must learn to appreciate our many practical conveniences.

Visiting Christian Churches in Communist China

First published in the Syracuse Post-Standard *on April 13, 1990.*

It was our first visit to a Christian church in northern China. But even more important, it was the first time Mr. W, our young translator, had ever been in a Christian church in his life.

No one at the university professed Christianity, so we had a difficult time finding the Protestant church.

One Sunday, Bob and I took an early trolley-bus crowded with people to find the church. We thought we knew where it was, but we weren't sure. As we greeted people on the bus with our very limited Chinese, *ni hao* (hello), they'd smile and return our greeting. But one woman noticed my Bible in my pocket. She pointed to the

Bible and nodded, pointing to her bag, too. She made the sign of the cross and said, "Jesu," I nodded, making a similar sign. She pointed to herself and said something in Chinese.

A young girl standing nearby told us in English that the woman said she, too, was a Christian and was going to the church. "If you're going to the church, just follow her." *Xie xie* (thank you). The door was opened for us.

We found there were three Christian churches in Harbin, a city of four million people—a Russian Orthodox, a Catholic, and a Protestant church. The Protestant church was a united Chinese church under the Chinese Christian Three-Self Patriotic Movement (self administration, self support, self propagation). The churches must work closely with the "Religious Affairs Bureau" of the government, but they seem to be allowed freedom to worship as long as they stayed within the rules.

There were six hundred members of this Harbin Protestant church, and many, many more attending. They told me there were 170,000 "believers" in Harbin, the majority quietly and secretly worshipping in their homes. Each Sunday this lone Protestant church was over-crowded with worshippers at each of the three services, with people sitting in the aisles on tiny folding stools, on the stairs going up the balcony, and even two rows of worshippers sitting on the floor behind the pulpit and minister.

We couldn't understand the Chinese words, but we could get the spirit of the message. And we joined in loudly, singing in English as they sang "Holy, Holy, Holy" and "What a Friend We Have in Jesus" in Chinese.

Mr. W joined us at our second visit to a church. He was hesitant at first. He said he knew no "religious words," but he translated the sermon well. It was the story of the prodigal son. However, he said he was confused. He had many questions to ask, so on the bus home we talked. One word bothered him—something about three. Could the word be "trinity"?

"Yes, yes, that's the word—'trinity'—what does it mean?"

How does one explain the trinity to a young Chinese man who has no idea of Christianity? I tried to think how I had explained it to our children.

"Mr. W, you know that I'm a mother. We have two children."

"Oh, yes."

"But I'm also a wife. I'm Uncle Bob's wife."

"Yes, I know."

"And I'm also a sister. I have two brothers and two sisters, so I'm a sister to them. Do you understand?"

"Yes, I understand."

"I'm a mother, a wife, and a sister. Three separate titles with varying relationships and meanings to different people. Yet I'm just ONE person. Does that make sense to you?"

"Yes, I understand that."

"Well, that's similar to the trinity. It's God, Jesus, and the Holy Spirit—all separate, yet all ONE." And I tried to explain each. That seemed to satisfy him, but he asked for more.

"What is 'communion'? They said something about food and communion next Sunday. What does that mean?"

These questions weren't easy because I'm not a theological student, but I had to respond, for it took courage for him to ask. So I continued.

"Do you do things in memory of someone or in memory of a special event?"

"Oh yes, we celebrate many special events."

"Well, Christians remember Jesus' dying, giving his body and blood. We do this by taking a bit of bread and a sip of juice or wine. It is to remind us of his sacrifice, helping us to rededicate our lives to God's work. Understand?"

"Yes, I understand. But I have another word, 'baptism.' The man said, 'Jesus was baptized, and we are baptized.' What does that mean?"

"'Baptism' or 'christening.' Water is sprinkled on your head as a symbol that your life is dedicated to God and his work. So, it's sort of a dedication or rededication ceremony, with water. Does that make sense?"

I wondered. Did he understand, or was he merely being polite, as all Chinese are? As I thought it over, I tried to think of other ways to define these words that we Christians know so well and say so glibly. Could I have done it better?

That night, Mr. W came to our small apartment, hesitantly asking if he could read my Bible. It is the *Good News New Testament*, written simply with stick-figure drawings. He had looked over my shoulder in church and evidently wanted to know more. Bibles were scarce in northern China.

We met one young man when we visited the Russian Orthodox Church. He spoke quietly to me, had seen us at the Protestant Church, maybe even followed us. Mr. L was twenty-three years old, from a nearby university, coming originally from a nearby small village.

Mr. L explained that in a village, outside of staying to work as a peasant worker, there were only two things a boy could do—join the army or pass the examination for the university. It was very difficult for a village boy to pass the national university entrance examination because only 20 percent pass and the village schools were quite backward. But he passed. A former teacher at the university gave him a Chinese Bible, but it was difficult for him to read and understand. He wanted to know more.

And music! The loudspeakers at the university blast out at 6 a.m.—mostly classical music and some martial music, but when I heard the music of "Jesu, Joy of Man's Desire," I looked around in astonishment. No one seemed to know the words or the message. And on a Chinese TV commercial for skin cream, comparing it to pearls, the background music was, of all things, "Amazing Grace."

We had three offers from people to go to church with us, to translate. Many Chinese were hesitant to attend church because they knew the government frowned on attendance, even though everyone was free to worship. However, many Chinese were curious—what better way to get into a church and see and hear for themselves, with government not disapproving, than by going as a translator for a foreign guest?

I went to a mosque in Harbin with a Muslim friend during Ramadan, the month of fasting and prayer, where there were a thousand people in attendance. I was told there were over thirty thousand Muslems in Harbin. And we went to a Taoist Temple and a Buddhist Temple, both active but with limited worshippers. We attended the Catholic Church with hundreds crowding the service, learning that there was an underground Roman Catholic Church that continued contact with Rome. Christians, Buddhists, and Muslims do have freedom to worship, but openly being "religious" means that job opportunities are limited.

Dancing and TaiJi Quan at Dawn

First published in the Syracuse Post-Standard *on May 2, 1990.*

Dawn in cold Harbin, China, is a busy time. Music blared from the university loudspeaker as workers, professors, and students diligently exercised in so many ways.

On our sturdy black Chinese bicycles, Bob and I wove around hundreds of joggers in colorful outfits, small groups of elderly men and women walking in their baggy dark pants and Mao jackets and caps, vigorous young people slashing at flying shuttlecocks as they played badminton right on the walkways. Others were walking among the trees or sitting on benches reading aloud in English, in Russian, in Japanese—a practical way to practice speaking their second languages.

As we neared the library, we heard an amplified tape recording giving the directions for Chinese disco dancing. During the winter, perhaps 100 to 150 gathered, but now that spring was coming there were well over 200 in the class, the overflow standing in lines on the frozen ground.

Clothing varied—colorful sweaters and scarves on some of the students, sturdy hand-knit jacket sweaters in dark blues and maroons on the older women, and many of the men workers in Mao jackets and caps. We all looked heavy and sturdy, but it was because we were all "layered" to keep warm.

There was always a leader. In our exercise group, she stood on the platform entrance to the library, three steps up so we could all see her. She exercised with her back to us so we could follow more easily.

Then came Chinese disco, which seemed to be replacing the traditional TaiJi Quan. It's a combination of many things. Some of the motions are similar to TaiJi Quan but faster and in rhythm, a modification of some American disco and even some heel-toe steps of the American square dance.

As we exercised in rhythm to the music, other activities were going on. A stooped sweeper pushed her crude broom as she swept the street. A youngster, perhaps three years old, darted between the disco dancers, the proud and lenient grandfather having little control.

After a half-hour of disco, the tape was changed. One morning it was cha-cha-cha, and a middle-aged Chinese woman grabbed me and we danced. She was a dancer and a strong leader, and we were the "hit" of the morning, with many "thumbs up" signs and murmurs of *Hao* (good).

There were small groups doing TaiJi Quan all over the campus. This is the ancient slow rhythmic dance form with bent knees and precise movements. You learn to relax and forget yourself in this thousand-year-old practice and its traditional shadow boxing exercises.

Over in the field by the library there were perhaps a dozen rhythmically and slowly doing the graceful TaiJi Quan. I made my way to join them, for I wanted so badly to learn TaiJi, which is much more difficult than Chinese disco. It takes years to learn all eighty-eight movements; I learned only the first thirteen. The Chinese insisted it was good for your health in many ways—blood pressure, arthritis, back problems—and I must admit it made me feel good.

I followed the leader as best I could, with encouragement from the other participants. But the leader saw my need for help and took me aside at the conclusion of the group exercise to work with me on the basic steps. Even after several weeks I learned only the basics, and my knees ached because of the strain on them, keeping them in a slightly bent position throughout the TaiJi.

And TaiJi is always followed by ballroom dancing. Yes, at the crack of dawn, even on the coldest days, from fox trot and waltz to cha-cha-cha. Most Chinese are graceful and excellent dancers.

Great exercise, a socializing time, and for me, a way to meet new friends and become a part, even for a few months, of the real Chinese life. How grateful I was that they included me so graciously—hospitable Chinese indeed!

A Women's College in Southern China: Fuzhou, 1994

Fuzhou is on the southern coast of China, on the Ming River, halfway between Shanghai and Hong Kong, nearly directly across from Taiwan. It is only an hour by plane from Hong Kong, but at the time of our visit, they were two different worlds. Fuzhou was a city of two million people and almost no Westerners. There were no English signs, and no English was spoken on the streets. We were indeed illiterate in this part of China.

We had been invited to work in the English Department of Hwa Nan Women's College in Southern China. The college was founded in 1911 with the support of the Methodist Missionary Societies. It was one of China's first women's colleges. The State University of New York had accredited it in 1922, and it had a strong academic reputation at the time, especially its English department. Then in 1950 the Communist government took over all educational institutions, including the women's college, which ended up merged with other institutions. The college was no more.

Thirty-five years later, in 1985, a group of dedicated and capable alumnae revived the college and its spirit of serving others, with Professor R, who was in her nineties, as its president. Starting with nothing—no land, no buildings, no government support— these women, all in their sixties, seventies, and eighties, followed their dreams.

The father of one alum contributed an old building. The women turned it into classrooms, with only themselves as resources and teachers. They found a wealthy Hong Kong businessman who had grown up in Fuzhou. Mr. S was a dedicated Buddhist who believed in helping others, especially in the area of education, and he wanted to help the women's college. Mr. S told other successful Hong Kong businessmen about the college's history, suggesting that they join him on a board of trustees to help support the college.

The women administrators realized they needed even more help. So Professor R, the president of the women's college, and Professor H, the head of the English Department—the only Christians and the only ones who spoke English—went to America in the mid-1980s to arrange support from American churches.

With limited funds, these dedicated Chinese women secured an architect and supervised the construction of their new classroom building. Remember, this was the only private women's college in all of China. It received no government support, and its graduates would land no government jobs. The graduates would have to find their own jobs—a new concept in China.

As we approached the small campus, we passed a wall where all notices for the four departments were posted. In the Food and Nutrition Department, the students were taught to cook and bake for institutions and restaurants. They operated their own tiny restaurant and bakery, which brought income to the college.

In the Clothing and Design Department, the girls learned practical skills, such as cutting cloth, as well as how to create their own designs. The graduating class gave a runway show so professionally done that local TV stations broadcast it throughout the province. On the heels of that success, job offers started coming in.

The Child Care Department was most important, especially with China's one-child-per-family policy.

The fourth department at the college was the English Department. A big problem was that by long practice, China's schools had taught the *reading* and *writing* of English and neglected *listening* and *speaking* skills. My assignment was to work with the Chinese teachers, realigning their work and showing the importance of teaching all four skills—listening, speaking, reading, and writing—in sequence.

How Do You Communicate Without a Common Language?

As we walked through a nearby park early one morning, we heard music. We followed the sounds and found a group of retirees. We learned that they met each morning for impromptu concerts of traditional music with ancient instruments, reliving earlier days through song and dance. They welcomed us, offering us a seat on a rock wall nearby. They seemed delighted to have an audience and responded enthusiastically to our applause and smiles of delight.

As I sat quietly, enjoying the music, a tiny Chinese woman wearing Mao pants and jacket touched me on the arm. I looked up with a smile, wondering what she wanted. She smiled back, and seemed to be digging into her deep pockets. Did she want money? Did she feel I should pay something for enjoying this concert? I waited.

She pulled out some crumbled Chinese bills, then shook her head and put the bills back. I didn't understand why she kept touching my arm, keeping my attention from the musicians.

Then came a big grin—she had found what she was looking for. In her hand was a tiny wooden cross. She pointed at the cross, then at herself, nodding her head, saying something in Chinese. I assumed she was telling me she was a Christian. Then she pointed at me and at the cross, a questioning look on her face—she was asking if I was a Christian, too. I nodded my head, pointed at the cross, and gave a big smile, assuring her that I, too, was Christian. We hugged, and everyone in the group clapped.

Yes, we had communicated, even without a common language.

Lost: What to Do?

First published in the Syracuse Post-Standard *on July 14, 1994.*

We were lost in an unfamiliar area of crowded Fuzhou!

We stood for a few moments after getting off the bus, searching for just one familiar feature—a street, a building, or even a Chinese sign we'd seen before. We recognized nothing. How could we find our way back? We couldn't ask or even understand directions for we couldn't understand or speak Chinese. Not being able to read Chinese made all the signs look alike to us.

Bob and I had taken the over-packed, run-down No. 1 bus to the downtown area of Fuzhou and confidently took the No. 1 bus back. We didn't know that the second bridge across the Ming River was being repaired and was closed to returning buses. Bus No. 1 had taken a detour.

Our only hope of getting back "home" was pointing to our little Chinese pins with the name of our school and shrugging our shoulders, hoping someone would point us in the right direction. Two hours of walking, zig-zagging back and forth as individual Chinese directed us, we finally made our way back to the women's college that was our "home" in Southern China.

China and the United States are comparable in size, but in 1990, China had 1.2 billion people, while the United States had 250 million. With 5 billion people in the world, that meant that one out of every 5 persons in the world was Chinese. And yet how little we know of China, its people, its customs, its history, its traditions.

Most transportation in Fuzhou was by bicycle. Thousands of bicycles—with identical tingling bells, built-in locks, no reflectors—stream by, often ten deep. When it rained, each rider dug in his pocket for the ever-ready plastic cape. Many rode tandem—one pedaling and the other perched carefully over the rear fender.

Mini-motorbikes were fashionable, and we saw helmeted drivers weaving in and out among the bicyclists. They also served as instant taxi service when buses broke down—and that was often.

One Fuzhou friend took all his savings out of the bank to purchase a minibike. Prices had tripled, and he was afraid to wait any longer. However, he had a problem. He couldn't get a license. The government was concerned that too many motorbikes on the roads would make traffic impossible. So it had limited the number of licenses issued monthly. How did one get on the list? Unless you had *guangxi*—connections—your name continually went to the bottom of the list.

Buses were second in serving the people's transportation demands. Waiting in crowded bus stops was easy compared to pushing your way onto the bus. The Chinese people were generally polite and hospitable, but not when it came to getting on or off buses. They pushed, shoved, and elbowed their way on.

The streets were always crowded with vendors carrying produce balanced on bamboo poles slung over their shoulders. Sturdy shoes were needed, for walking was still the main way to get to the tiny markets and shops to fulfill daily needs.

An Orphanage and an Old Folks' Home

The Chinese love children, but with the tremendous population explosion and limited land and facilities, the government strictly enforced a one-child-per-family policy.

Everyone worked in China, so most children were cared for by their grandparents. Education was free and had a high priority. Teachers were greatly respected, though their salaries were low. Children were given the best a family could afford, as was clear from their general good health and colorful outfits.

How is the government able to enforce a one-child-per-family policy? Peer pressure is one way, and another is easily available contraceptive measures. But what happens if a woman conceives and the parents decide to keep the second child?

The second child does not get free education or health care. The parents can lose their jobs or the prospects for promotion. In the villages, some parents "hide" their second babies, but it is harder to do in the city. The decision parents face is never easy: Do they abort the second child? Do they try to keep it? Do they give it away after it's born?

Traditionally, Chinese took care of second or third children in their extended family system, but with two- or three-room apartments and no one to look after them, and especially under the single-child law, that was no longer possible.

In Fuzhou, we visited a large orphanage, where few visitors were welcome. It was austere but clean, operated by loving attendants clad in white. The facilities were adequate, the toys colorful. There was even individual potty training.

Who were these children, and why had they been left here? I had expected to see mostly girls because of the Chinese culture's strong yearning for sons. Instead, I saw equal numbers of boys and girls. Some of the children were deformed or had mental or emotional problems that were too much for poor, hard-working parents to handle. Some parents found that they couldn't take care of even a healthy second child. The children were seldom adopted, but they did receive loving care here.

What about the old folks, the very elderly in China? Many grandparents live in extended families, for they're needed to care for their grandchildren. But more and more elderly people are living out their autumn years in old folks homes.

On a narrow street near our school was an old folks home. All the people there were in their eighties or nineties, wearing the traditional and comfortable Mao pants and jackets. An old, gnarled tree had been on the property for one hundred years, and with the Chinese love of nature and the need for shade, it had been decided that the facilities would be built around the tree.

There was a tiny TV room, popular when the electricity was on, and an alcove where the residents could play their favorite games. Red signs with Chinese characters gave greetings at each door. Each person had a bed with mosquito netting and a corner in a tiny room for personal possessions, with simple traditional facilities for cooking. All these folks received a very small monthly government check as pensioners that covered their living expenses there. Loneliness was their biggest problem, for they received few visitors, and the families were usually far away.

Family Life

We were invited to several Chinese homes for dinner. Typically, a family of four—a grandparent, the parents, and one child—lives in two or three rooms in an austere apartment house. There are very few individual homes in China.

One of the Chinese teachers at a women's college in Southern China, Professor T, invited us to dinner at her traditional Chinese home. Decades ago, it had been a home for an extended family, with each son having a few rooms for his own family. By the time of our visit it had been divided into smaller units, but the courtyard must have been elegant in its day.

The grandfather greeted us by offering a bowl of water for us to wash our hands. The grandmother had prepared and served a simple meal, and the six of us crowded around the tiny table, eating in the typical Chinese way, using chopsticks and eating from a common bowl.

The young couple shared a bedroom with the baby and shared the traditional kitchen with Professor T's in-laws. Up a set of creaking stairs was the grandparents' room, where they shared a small bed under mosquito netting. The back door opened to a tiny yard with a deep well where they drew their own water—something few families could do these days.

Professor T had been to college in America, spoke and taught English, and was a modern, up-to-date Chinese professional, but she was also a traditional wife and mother. Once home, she lived with her husband's parents, who had taken over the responsibility of raising their son.

One of the vice presidents of a women's college, unmarried, was fortunate to have her own three-room apartment—a real luxury. The college administrators met at her home each week to prepare and enjoy together a traditional Chinese meal. We were flattered to be included.

It was a fun day as they showed us how to make their special dumplings, packing themselves into the tiny kitchen to do the necessary preparations. Afterwards we crowded around the round table, enjoying the food and the companionship even though we had no common language, using chopsticks and Chinese bowls with our wonderful hostesses.

Christianity, Buddhism, Ancestor Worship, and Turning Back to Old Gods

Under communist rule in China, all religions were denounced, and atheism was declared official policy. During the Cultural Revolution, all church and religious buildings were taken over by the government and converted into factories, warehouses, office buildings, or flats. It meant that most of the old church buildings that were given back to the Christians were not in good repair when we visited them in 1990.

There was freedom of religion by that year, but it was not encouraged, and believers found it hard to find work. Even so, the Protestant and Catholic churches were crowded every Sunday morning, with worn pianos played loudly to accompany enthusiastic singing. At one time only the elderly had attended services, but no more—by 1990, hundreds of young adults were attending.

Pastor Want well remembered one day during the Cultural Revolution. He had been leading his choir in the church when the Red Guards burst in. They handcuffed him and made him kneel down before them and "confess" that he was teaching the choir untruths when he was teaching of God. The young guards struck him, spat on him, kicked him, and threw him in jail, where he remained for five years. Then he endured another five years' hard labor in the villages.

Pastor Want had a hard time forgiving these young people, but his faith kept him going. In 1990, when he grew discouraged, he sang. Music gave him the strength to endure, he said. Life hadn't been easy for Christians in China, especially during the Cultural Revolution, but things were slowly changing.

So, there *was* religious freedom in China in 1990. But could one really say it was *free* when people found their careers threatened because of their beliefs? By then, Christianity was growing tremendously in China within the Three-Self Patriotic Movement. But I was told that the "underground church"—those who quietly and secretly worshipped in small groups in their homes—was growing even more.

Buddhism continued to be the major religion of China, and huge, colorful paper wreaths were still being sold in the markets for funeral services.

Ching Ling Day continued to be the day for remembering one's ancestors. Tiny Buddhist shops sold incense, colorful banners, and paper money. Believers burned the paper money and paper replicas of worldly goods, in the belief that they would then journey to the next world for their departed loved ones. At home, tables were set with favorite foods for the ancestors, and candles were lit. Both these customs were thousands of years old. And in the corner of one room in a house, there was always a small altar on which were placed incense and fruit. Ancestor worship continued to be strong in rural China.

The most active Buddhist temple in Fuzhou was a magnificent red-and-gold temple on Mount Drum. The entrance was guarded by huge stone lions, and priests watched over the entrance to the throne room of their smiling Golden Buddha. Drums beat and gongs sounded as yellow-robed priests chanted and prayed, letting all know that believers continued to practice their religious rites and traditions. In small alcoves, elderly priests continued to teach novices and wise old men continued reading and studying from ancient scrolls and books.

Many Chinese continue worship of their ancestors, and some have turned back to old gods. To visit Ling Wua, the Goddess of the Island, the protector of fishermen and travelers, we joined hundreds of devotees on a crowded ferry to the tiny fishing village of Mei Zhou, where ancient Chinese temples rise up the hills.

In 1994, thousands of Chinese came from all parts of China to celebrate the thousandth anniversary of Ling Wua's birth. The red tile roofs of temple buildings shone in the brilliant sunlight. Firecrackers boomed and smoke rose as incense was burned and pigs and goats were sacrificed. Worshippers knelt in prayer to colorful gods, and finally to the two hundred-foot-high goddess, Ling Wua.

Yes, religion is still alive in China.

Ecuador and Peru, 1987 and 1988

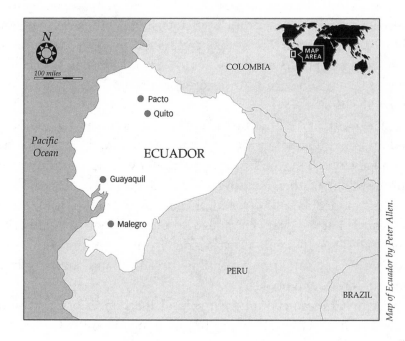

Map of Ecuador by Peter Allen.

Ecuador is a small country in the northwest corner of South America, a democracy, right on the equator, hot and humid on the coast, perfect weather in the mountain area, and rainforest in the Amazon—and, of course, the astonishing Galapagos Islands.

An invitation to do volunteer work in a developing country from the International Executive Service Corps is highly prized, but it also entails long hours of demanding work, and detailed reporting is expected. We were delighted to be invited by the IESC to go to Ecuador in 1987 and again in 1988. IESC is a prestigious organization, founded by Nelson Rockefeller and Harold McGraw in the early 1960s. It sends volunteer executives to companies in developing countries, with their wives, to help in their special field.

Guayaquil

Our main assignment was to be in Guayaquil. We had heard it rained heavily there, and as we looked out the plane window, we saw miles and miles of land under water. We had no idea there would also be floods. We soon learned that it rained every night and often during the day and that the sun, when it appeared, brought high humidity.

We saw few tourists, for this was an industrial city, with sidewalks and streets in constant disrepair. I felt tall (even though I'm only five feet two), for most of the indigenous people were nearly a head shorter than I, with the mestizos (people of mixed blood) just a bit taller. In spite of the uneven sidewalks, most women wore high heels to look taller. Ecuadorians come in all shades, from dark brown to chocolate to light tan and white. Most have beautiful thick black hair.

I looked forward to meeting people. Some of my contacts were the parents of students at Syracuse University. That would give me opportunities to see both sides of this exciting city.

There was 50 percent unemployment in Guayaquil. Three or four families lived together, all trying to bring in a few *sucres*— the women and girls sold fruit, the boys shined shoes, the fathers picked up whatever odd jobs they could.

An Indigenous Corner Family

With 50 percent unemployment in Guayaquil, beggars were common on the hot, dirty streets. On most street corners were small families of Indians. The mother and children sat quietly in the hot tropical sun, selling fruit. These families spoke only Quechua and had recently arrived in the city in search of work and a better life.

I got to know the family on our hotel's corner, and just before we left the country I wanted to give the children balloons, Frisbees, and small toys, and to give some *sucres* to the mother. The children were delighted with the gifts, but a mestizo woman who sat nearby came up and took the gifts from the children and the mother. She said, in Spanish, "For me, for me." I tried to explain that they were for the children, but she got angrier: "For *me!*" That made me angry. I wasn't going to let her take them from the children, so I took the balloons, Frisbees, and toys back from the children. Their meek big eyes followed me.

I felt so ashamed. I hardly slept that night trying to figure out how to get the gifts to the children. A plan emerged. I brought a *big* bag of gifts, one or two for the mestizo woman, with duplicates for the Indian woman and children. As I quietly slipped the Indian woman some money, the mestizo woman eyed the gifts and allowed me to take pictures—but not of her.

This whole episode disturbed me. Is there a "boss system" even for the lowly Indians coming in? Or is this a system to protect the newcomer Indians who speak no Spanish, to give them a livelihood even in the early days in a new city?

Guasmos: Just One Barrio

One of the poorest neighborhoods of Guayaquil was in the Guasmos, a barrio called "Union de Bananeros No. 1." In dry weather the streets were passable; during the rainy season they were deep mud. Most of the homes were bamboo huts, haphazardly built and each housing a family of from five to ten. The people were squatters, and each family had built its own simple house, paying seven hundred *sucres* a month for electricity. The only water available was brought by truck and cost sixty *sucres* a barrel. In spite of the poverty, everything seemed clean, and there were no bad odors—except at the entrance of the barrio, where there was a garbage dump. The garbage was supposed to be collected by the government, but they seldom got around to it.

Our good friends Mickey and Jim Reynolds had supported a family here through the Foster Children's Plan. Maria, age fourteen, was their adopted daughter. She and her brother and sisters lived with their grandparents. Maria was in the first year of high school and felt lucky, for with her adopted parents' help she was able to take the bus to school instead of walking. High school classes are held only in the afternoon because the same building was used for morning classes for the little ones, six to twelve years old. Their hut was made entirely of bamboo matting—the flooring, the sides, the roof. It was immaculately clean and orderly, with household items hanging on the walls. I saw only the one mattress in the corner.

Maria and her grandmother cooked for the family on a simple stove using bottled gas. Clothes were always drying on the tiny mud-floored patio at the back. Grandma pointed with pride to the latrine, a cement block outhouse, their latest addition. She told me that it had been given to them by the Plan Internationale.

Foreigners seldom come to the Guasmos, and at least fifteen children and over a dozen mothers flocked around to look us over. The social worker for Plan Internationale had 170 families to care for—an astonishing workload. She explained that the Foster Children's Plan, the Plan Internationale, allowed donors to adopt one child. But if all the funds went only to that one child, how would the rest of the family and the neighbors feel? So the agreement was that Maria herself would get special help, but part of the funds would go directly to her family (that's how they got their new latrine), and another part to the village (that's how they got the paved road). That way, everyone gained—Maria was helped, her family was helped, and the village was helped—and no one resented Maria's special assistance.

The Reynoldses could be proud of Maria, who lived in such poverty yet was rich in love and joyous in her pursuit of her studies.

Quito: Centro del Muchachos Trabajadores

In 1962 an American priest named Father Halligan came to Ecuador and with Sister Miguel started Centro del Muchachos Trabajadores (Center for Working Boys). At the time, hundreds of small boys were wandering the streets, trying to earn a few *sucres* by shining shoes. Father Halligan and Sister Miguel had been assigned to help these boys. Over the years, Father Halligan and Sister Miguel realized that they couldn't work with these boys in isolation: they would have to work with entire families.

The rules were strict for the Centro del Muchachos families. All members had to belong as a unit, and each member had to find some useful work—no idleness permitted. A tiny percentage of the income of each member *had* to be saved, and the center banked for these people to make sure it was done. There was no welfare or social security in Ecuador.

All of the family, mother and father as well as children, had to be attending some sort of education. The children had to be going to school. If the parents weren't working, the man had to be learning a trade. The women might be learning to sew, right there at the center.

Cleanliness was mandatory, and poverty was no excuse. If someone said, "But we're so poor—there is no water in our hut," that excuse was not accepted, for Centro had its own showers. You signed in by making the first half of an X— / —after your name as you took the soap and towel, then finished the X as you returned the soap and towel. No shower meant no food and no classes.

Attendance at some religious service, not necessarily Catholic, was required. Work, cleanliness, education, and some kind of moral or faith community were all essential, for these were the basis of a solid family and community.

I was deeply impressed with their program, but how could I help? Their answer: they had trade classes for adults and school classes for the children, but they had no classes for adults who couldn't read or write in Spanish. Working as a team, we developed basic Spanish literacy books, and I made new friends.

The Center worked with seventy-five families—outstanding work. If only this kind of program could be expanded throughout the country!

Ladrones: The Thieves' Market

Most Ecuadorians are gracious hosts, helping foreigners whenever possible. But Ecuador also has its *ladrones*—its outlaws and thieves. We were cautioned never to wear jewelry or carry a purse.

We visited the big market near San Francisco Cathedral in Old Quito. Some call it "the thieves' market." I wore no jewelry and kept my camera and journal under my jacket. Bob's only money was in a money belt.

We found the cathedral and the markets. Everyone we saw was in a festive mood. People were watching dancers; children were squirting soap and throwing water balloons and confetti. Indian women had booths selling candles, incense, and wood. As we walked on, we saw policemen directing heavy traffic on the narrow cobblestone streets. Finally we came to the big market, where chickens, vegetables, fruit, and whole smoked pigs were for sale.

The crowd grew more dense, and I tried to hang on to Bob's arm, but the Indian and mestizo women pushed and shoved, finally separating the two of us. I saw tiny Indian women with black felt hats, strings of colorful beads, and long, full, bright skirts and ponchos, some carrying tiny babies on their backs, and many mestizos. But I could not see Bob.

I finally saw him at the edge of the crowd, laughing hysterically. He lifted his jacket and showed me a cut in the front of his trousers about three inches long. It seems that two tiny Indian women, wrapped in shawls, had jostled him, pushing him from behind and in front. As a gentleman, he tried to let them pass. It all happened so quickly. They felt his money belt and tried to take it. The razor went through his jacket, trousers, shirt, and even his underwear. What saved him from being cut was his money pouch. We both looked closer—there was a five-inch cut in the back of his jacket. He was wearing a small backpack (with our rain gear), and evidently they had thought there was money in there, too.

Bob hadn't noticed a thing until he felt the hole in his trousers. Those two women had been real professionals.

One Person's Work in One Poor Village

We first met the Reverend Margaret Kreller when she spoke at the Interdenominational Church in Quito. We were impressed by her concern for the forgotten people on the coast of Ecuador, in Malegro, who were flooded out every year.

Malegro was an old, dilapidated city on the Pacific coast. Margaret lived on a tiny farm nearby and was trying, through example and hard work, to bring community development and better nutrition to the people there. She had built a simple concrete house several years earlier, with an outhouse and outdoor shower, for she knew she would have to protect her health if she was to do any good there. She hoped that her project might serve as a model.

It was mid-afternoon when we left in Margaret's truck to attend a meeting of local workers. Flooding was bad that year—in six places along our route, the road had been washed away. Our destination was an old school where fourteen men and three women, representatives of six areas, were meeting. Over the years Margaret had encouraged them to gather to discuss their problems and develop action plans instead of lethargically accepting their fate.

Working together, they had gotten electricity for five of the six villages. Electricity? I looked up and saw a single lightbulb. That was their electricity. But how to get electricity in the sixth village? One village working alone got nothing. They were learning that by sticking together, they'd more likely get electricity for *all* the villages.

In all six villages, wells had been dug, but the water was being pulled up one bucket at a time. They needed water pumps—even hand pumps—and they had called the meeting to start planning how to get them.

It was hot and humid, and I was constantly mopping my face. But it was when I crossed my legs and they squished back and forth, as in a sauna, that I realized how hot and humid it really was. And it was that way all the time in Malegro.

It had taken Margaret more than five years to gain the trust of the people here, to instill in them the fact that six villages had more power than one, to encourage them to set communal goals and work out solutions. Who said life was easy? It wasn't here in Malegro, but the people were proud that they were working together.

Pastor Sergio Gonzales in Faraway Pacto

When we travel to a new place, I try to gather the names of as many local contacts as I can. One of the names given to me by the Presbyterian Church was Pastor Sergio Gonzales. We met, and he invited us to visit his church outside Quito. I assumed that it was a suburban church and was amazed to find that though Pacto was only a hundred kilometers from the city, it took five hours of rugged driving to get there.

Loaded with sleeping bags, bottled water, and food, we started off in our rented car with Pastor Sergio driving. Because he usually took the bus and spent three days there, his family had never visited his Pacto church. He had neglected to tell us that he'd invited them to come with us and that there'd be six of us plus baggage in a tiny car meant for four.

Over narrow, winding dirt roads, we wound our way through the mountains, up, down, and around, staring down steep cliffs, seeing Ecuador in all its spectacular beauty.

Pacto is a village of a thousand people—or two thousand, depending on whom you talk to. It was founded eighty to ninety years ago, after a group of mestizos walked several days from Quito and chose this spot for their new home. They hacked fields out of the jungle for cropland, acquired some animals, built huts, found water, and by the time of our visit had electricity. They were rightfully proud of their village.

Ecuador is a religious country, close to 100 percent Catholic, but we were to visit a tiny Protestant church in Pacto. Pastor Sergio hoped we would arrive in time for the Sunday service, but Latin Americans are casual about time, so the fact that we were an hour late for the service made little difference. When word got out that visitors had arrived, the forty or so members of the Pacto Evangelical Church, including children, gathered to worship.

The eight crude wooden pews, four on each side of the simple wooden structure, began to fill. The village itself was predominantly mestizo; the Indians, who lived high in the mountains, walked down to the village for Sunday services.

One mestizo and his tiny Indian wife walked many miles each Sunday from their shack for morning service, then walked home afterwards. The wife in her Indian shawl kept looking at me, and I'd smile, and she'd grin, with no front teeth. I wished we could communicate and share experiences.

The service opened with prayer and readings from the Bible— all in Spanish—led by seventeen-year-old Patricio. The reading was followed by a heartfelt sermon from Pastor Sergio. Then followed singing and clapping, accompanied by Sergio on an accordion, Patricio on a guitar, and the local schoolteacher on an ancient drum. Music was important in this remote village, where there was little other entertainment.

Not until later did I learn that the accordion and the guitar were only on loan to this church, for a month. Many tiny churches had to share them. Pastor Sergio explained that sharing these instruments was worth the effort, for music meant so much to the villagers. Their dream was to have their own accordion or their own guitar someday so that they could have music weekly or even daily.

Mario, the lay leader, had invited us to eat with his family. I had brought a chicken wrapped in ice in a plastic bag, plus potatoes and Coke, knowing that these folks couldn't afford guests. But we, with the Gonzales family, were their guests, crowding into their tiny tin-roofed, cement-block house, sitting on boxes around a larger crate covered with a white cloth. Their warmth and hospitality made for a happy meal. It's sad that their smiles were always through tight lips. Because of poor nutrition, most had lost their front teeth by the time they were twenty years old.

We wandered through the streets of Pacto, feeling the stares of the curious, for no North Americans had ever visited their village. The church members decided we should stay in their one-room hospital, which was empty at the time. The bed was made of wooden slats and barely wide enough for our two sleeping bags. We weren't there for comfort, and the view from the screenless open window was spectacular.

The next day Bob and I got out our Frisbees. Bob started with two children, then eight, then sixteen, with the elders sitting on the stoop or leaning out windows, laughing and enjoying it all. We had two Frisbees, and eventually both were on a roof. The children scurried around for a bamboo ladder and a pole and got them down. Everyone joined in the fun, and not only the children of the church families, for more people kept arriving. I guess the word had got around that gringos were there.

The children would come and sit by me, and we would start games and songs. We counted in Spanish and English: one little, two little, three little children—*uno pecena, dos pecena, tres pecena niños*. Then we sang "This Little Light of Mine" with gestures.

Bob got a drum from the church and started a parade, with the children lined up behind him as if he were the Pied Piper, all saying in English "left, right, left, right." The children loved it, as did the parents.

We had promised to be back at the church for services, for Pastor Sergio had asked me to give a simple first lesson in reading and writing in both Spanish and English. I was prepared.

More people kept coming. Soon the four pews on each side were full, with more people standing at the back. Patricio opened with prayer; that was followed by enthusiastic singing accompanied by Sergio and his accordion, Patricio with his guitar, and the teacher on the drums. It was a fun time.

Then came my turn. Sergio translated, saying they might want to know how "Aunt Ruth" taught. I showed a picture of a typical Spanish village, asking if it looked familiar. Yes, they told me, it did. When I asked for one word to describe it, they talked among themselves and decided on the word *familia*. I wrote it on the board and broke it into syllables, continuing with teaching the sounds of a-e-i-o-u and building new syllables from them. They loved it and responded well, not just the children but the parents, too.

Then Sergio explained that I'd give the first lesson in English. I began by standing up as I said "Stand up." Everyone laughed and stood up—they understood. Then "sit down." Next, because I had colored balloons for the children, we worked on colors.

Patricio started his next part of the service by saying in English, "Stand up." How they laughed as they all stood up to sing.

Everyone came to greet us, pleading with us to stay, saying that we could help them so much. They wanted Bob to set up a Sunday school, for the children loved him. They wanted me to teach, and the women wanted to talk more with me. They responded so warmly that I would have loved to stay there and teach.

We walked back to the hospital in the springlike air. There was an outside toilet and a water pipe. Yes, there was electricity, but that simply meant lightbulbs in some rooms. Our shuttered window was open, and we were sure that the one lightbulb in the ceiling would attract flies and mosquitoes. What a surprise—there were none!

We undressed and climbed into our sleeping bags, feeling fortunate to be welcomed so warmly by these people who had so little. Why were they born here and we in America? We certainly had done nothing to deserve our better life.

Sergio told us that most poor Ecuadorians felt that it was their fate to be poor. They believed they were helpless. He would tell them, "No, God loves you, and you can be more." Even so, it was often discouraging.

It surprised me how clean they kept themselves and their village despite the conditions they faced. There were no bad odors, and their bodies, hair, and clothes were all clean—which was hard work. The women were constantly sweeping out their huts and even sweeping the road in front of their huts.

We rose early to the crowing of roosters and the songs of birds, and rolled up our sleeping bags. Despite the wooden slats, we had slept well. As we washed at the pipe, we were constantly greeted with "Buenas dias, Tia Ruth y Tio Bob."

A church member lived next door. He invited us to his house, down crude steps to a simply made pigpen with two healthy pigs.

Chickens scratched in the yard. In the trees high above were pods a foot or two long, perhaps four inches wide and an inch thick. The man kicked off his rubber boots and, using only his feet and hands, scrambled up the tree. We clapped with surprise and delight. Using a long bamboo pole with a hook on the end, he reached way up and twisted a guava pod from the tree. This was a true guava— what Americans call guava Ecuadoreans call *guallava*. Each fruit has wide seeds about two inches long, perhaps ten to a pod. The outside is white and soft, the center dark brown and hard. You eat the white outer part, spitting out the big brown seeds. They were sweet and delicious.

Daily life was back on schedule. A woman was gathering scraps for her pigs; a man was working in his little shop. They had a school with a few teachers, but they needed books, slates, and pens and paper.

We had made good friends there and were "Tia Ruth" and "Tio Bob" to everyone in the village. The children gathered with their parents to say good-bye. I doubted we would ever see one another again, but we had gained much by witnessing their love and sharing. We knew we wouldn't forget them, but how could we help them? It is important just to share their story and to try to understand other cultures and people, but so often it doesn't seem like enough.

We were invited back to Ecuador the following year. I knew we'd never get to Pacto again, but I had shared Pastor Sergio's story with friends who had a guitar tucked somewhere in their attic. We gave it to Pastor Sergio, who shared the thanks of the villagers, telling us they would always think of us as they sang together.

Olga Fisch, Folklore Artist

I was walking up the main street toward the Intercontinental Hotel in Quito when coming toward me I saw an elderly aristocratic woman with a cane, holding onto the arm of a younger woman. We greeted each other—"Buenas dias"—and went on our way.

Perhaps an hour later I rang the bell of the beautiful and exclusive Olga Fisch Folklore Shop. To my surprise, one of the clerks hurried toward me, saying that Olga Fisch wanted to have coffee with me.

"Who, me? I don't know Olga Fisch."

"Yes you do—you and she greeted each other on the street."

Olga Fisch, by then a frail eighty-six-year-old, was an internationally known folklore artist who had designed rugs even for the United Nations. She had known as soon as we greeted each other on the street that I'd be coming to her shop. She insisted that that first encounter had been *brujeria* (witchcraft; fate). She *knew* I'd come to her shop, and she *knew* we'd become friends.

Olga was a charmer. She spoke six languages and had exhibited her art all over the world, including the Smithsonian Institution in Washington. She protected and fostered the folk art of Ecuador, which had been passed down from generation to generation. She had worked with the Ecuadorian Indians in the remotest areas,

30. *Olga Fisch was the internationally known folklore artist who brought Ecuadorian Indian art to the world.*

stressing quality work, and she had arranged for the best Ecuadorian artisans to weave her designs.

Dinner as Olga Fisch's guests was a highlight for us in Ecuador. She told us of her life in Hungary, Austria, Germany, Morocco, and Italy. In 1939, when it was no longer safe for Jews in Europe, she and her husband fled to the United States, only to find that the American quota for immigrants from Hungary had been filled for eighty-six years. That's when they applied for citizenship in Ecuador—the United States' loss and Ecuador's gain. Ecuador had been her home for over fifty years.

She shared stories of her early years in the villages of Ecuador, where she sought out folk artists, encouraging them to continue their work, giving them a way to make a living. A tour of her world-renowned collection of folk arts and crafts, and of her magnificent hand-woven wall hangings, gave us a real appreciation of this woman's creative gifts to the world. But it was one exquisite hanging of native Ecuadorian women that took my heart.

At our next meeting, Olga insisted that I have that special hanging. The price was far beyond our means, but she generously cut the price in half, telling us, "You're a new and special friend—you'll always care for this piece." Bob agreed, and that was a special birthday gift to me. It's still hanging in our living room.

Olga Fisch died, but her Folklore shops, her reputation as an internationally known artist, and her love and support of Ecuador's simple peasant crafts will remain.

Cuzco, Peru: A Padre's Story

While these stories are of Ecuador, another moving story was told to me in Cuzco, Peru.

In Cuzco, high in the Andes Mountains, in the land of the Incas, people still live as they did hundreds of years ago. Poverty, hard work, and a constant struggle to keep alive are the norm. While we were in Cuzco, a local priest heard of my interest in literacy and insisted I hear his story.

A local padre in a tiny mountain village was concerned about his people and wanted to help. But how? He experimented. During the rainy season he brought together fifteen men, village peasants. He never thought to include women, for women were considered workers and child bearers. They were not thought of as decision makers.

On the hard-packed dirt floor, the padre laid out a large piece of paper. He knew that none of the villagers could read or write. He handed the leader a large black crayon and then asked them to talk together and *draw* what they thought their village looked like. He reminded them to include themselves in the picture.

That was quite a challenge, and the men looked at each other, shrugging their shoulders. But their priest had asked them, so they huddled together and tried. They worked and worked, talked and discussed, changed and rearranged, and finally came up with a picture (see fig. 31).

31. First village drawing.

The men explained. The church was the center of their town, with the main road going by it. The padre was an important man. The big boss who owned most of the land was an important man, and his wife was important, too. They, the villagers, were smaller because they weren't so important. The big cows were owned by the big boss. The small cows were owned by the villagers.

The padre asked whether they'd like to learn to read any of the words indicated in their picture. A new idea! After much discussion, the men said they'd like to learn the following words:

man street rice
woman cow beans
father big boss banana
mother big house market
children little house money
padre work church

The padre taught the village men the words they wanted to learn, all words having to do with their everyday lives. But as the men talked, they became dissatisfied with their picture. They asked the padre if they could draw it again.

They drew what was generally the same picture of the village. But the padre noticed that the church wasn't quite as imposing. The padre and the big boss and his wife were still there, but now they were the same size as the villagers. There still was a difference in the sizes of the big boss's house and the villagers' houses, but the cows were the same size. The villagers were seeing themselves in a new light, and they knew more words that they wanted to learn. The padre was learning what was important to them by the words they wanted to learn.

One farmer wanted these words: *farm, cow, pigs, seeds.*

Another villager wanted these words: *doctor, sick, medicine, help.* The padre knew he had a sick child.

Yet another villager wanted these words: *roof, bricks, wood, window.* He was probably interested in building something.

Yet another wanted these words: *book, paper, pen, study.* Could it be that this was the beginning of interest in a school or education?

32. Revised village drawing.

Weeks went by, and the men gathered often to study and talk. Again they were dissatisfied with their village drawing. They decided they wanted to draw another picture of their village. This time they wanted to draw it as they hoped it would someday be (see fig. 32).

They wanted a school. They wanted piped water, sanitation, and roads that didn't turn to mud during the rainy season. This realistic thinking was the beginning of growth. They realized, too, that they must learn to read, and not just those words that were important to that lesson, but *all* words, so that they could learn to improve themselves, their children, and their village.

In Cuzco as in many villages of Peru, and in all of South America, they knew they'd have a long way to go, but they also knew that changes were coming. They saw their own needs and goals, and they knew they could work together to attain them.

⚁ Madagascar, 2000 and 2001

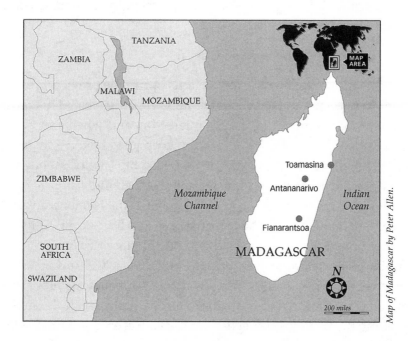

Map of Madagascar by Peter Allen.

We weren't sure where Madagascar was. It's the fourth-largest island in the world, one thousand miles long and five hundred miles wide, off the east coast of Africa.

Many millions of years ago it broke off from Africa, and more than two thousand years ago people of the Indonesian and Polynesian Islands came there, probably in outrigger canoes.

The people of Madagascar take pride in their Polynesian heritage, but now the Malagasy culture includes not just Polynesians, but also people of Indian, Indonesian, and African descent.

Bob and I were invited by the Northeast Synod Presbyterians USA to work with the Fiangonani Jesoa Kristy eto Madagasikara (FJKM—the Church of Jesus Christ in Madagascar). I would be training teachers to teach English as a second language, and also training them to teach reading and writing in Malagasy, the native language. Bob's project was to offer suggestions for soap saving and soap making. Soaps and detergents take a big share of family income, and Bob would be encouraging them to buy and sell detergent in bulk to save money.

Rice, the Staple Food of Madagascar

One farmer had harvested ten tons of rice the previous year. He needed two tons to feed his large family for the year. This farmer was strongly tempted to sell his huge crop, and when a local merchant offered to buy it, he decided to keep just one ton and sell the rest. He felt rich and happy, for he had a big pile of money with which to pay his bills and buy gifts for himself and his family.

After a few months, the rice was gone, so the farmer went to the merchant to buy more. The price had gone up 50 percent. At the end of more months the farmer had to buy still more rice at a price now double his original selling price, and again at well over 125 percent. He was buying back his own rice at a tremendous profit to the merchant. Of course he was upset, but he hadn't seen the logic of keeping the two tons he needed for his family each year and selling only the extra tons for profit. It takes education and often expensive lessons to change traditional ways.

Rice is Madagascar's staple food, and most of the time, the island grows enough rice to feed itself. But often, cyclones strike the island, bringing torrential rains that rot much of the rice in the fields. The orange clay soil is excellent for rice growing, but it is also good for the simple bricks used for most buildings. Because of the instant cash they can get for their orange clay for bricks, each year the rice farmers dig deeper into their rice paddies, pulling out more topsoil, shaping it and baking the bricks in crude ovens. Over the years they've been losing much of the rich red clay. All of this has added to the perennial problem facing many small rice farmers like Mr. Rajaonary—they don't know how to plan ahead for their personal needs. As a result, they sell their entire crop at harvest time and end up having to repurchase their own rice.

Prisons in Madagascar

I've visited prisons in America as well as in other countries, but prisons in Madagascar were beyond miserable. Throughout this poor country there was hope, but we also encountered despair when we visited two prisons.

Corruption was rampant, with bribery the general rule. Security was tight, and because of the poor conditions, few were allowed to visit—especially *vazahas* (the Malagasy word for white foreigners). We were fortunate to be allowed to visit after our passports and visas were examined and we gained the approval of the prison authorities.

First we visited the men's prison. There were no individual cells; everyone was behind thick walls and iron gates, living together in crowded rooms with no lights and with slits for windows. They were not restricted to specific rooms but roamed around the open dirt-floored area—no privacy here. All the men seemed lethargic, and we could sense their lack of hope.

The FJKM Mamre Sisters, a group of devout women who were devoting their lives to helping others, had brought in several huge bags of rice and greens, and several men immediately put pots of water on to boil. Mealtime was whenever food arrived, and there was never enough of it.

Several hundred men gathered to look at us, for we were a real curiosity. The head man—was he a guard or one of the prisoners?—explained our visit and invited me to speak to them. Through an interpreter, I gave greetings from America, describing ourselves as parents and grandparents and saying how much we liked their country, especially the people, who had been so kind to us (to which they applauded). Trying to show similarities, I said there were problems in Madagascar, but there were also problems in America, that we must help each other (more applause). Because of my concern for

33. *Hope seems lost in the men's prison in Madagascar, who looked forward only to the time the Mamre Sisters brought food.*

literacy, I asked whether anyone wanted to learn to read in Malagasy. Perhaps half the men raised their hands. Those who could read—did they have any books? No. Would they like some? In French or Malagasy? "Malagasy!" they called out. It was so sad that there were no books and no classes and that no one seemed to care. These men felt forgotten.

From there, we visited the women's prison. We saw much more activity there. Women were washing clothes, hanging them to dry

34. *Women seem to adapt to prison life better than men, for there is activity here with jobs that must be done for themselves and the children.*

on a clothesline. Charcoal fires were being lit to cook rice. There were babies and young children—always signs of hope. If a woman was pregnant when she came to jail, she was treated just like the rest. But once she started labor, she was taken to a nearby hospital for the traditional birthing. Then she and the baby were returned to jail to await trial or to complete her sentence.

Six young women, probably sixteen to eighteen years of age, were in a makeshift schoolroom with an older woman acting as teacher. They had only finished primary school. They had been here less than six months, but they already realized that without education they were doomed. One was in for murder—having been beaten and abused by her husband, she had killed him. Several were prostitutes. Others were accused of theft. One young girl had been a maid in a wealthy family's house. A pen and a sheet were missing. Her boss accused her of stealing them, and even though she insisted she was innocent, she was in jail and had been for more than a year, awaiting a trial.

In Madagascar you were presumed guilty until you could prove your innocence. Yes, that's right—if someone accused you, you were jailed immediately and often waited five to ten years for a trial. One woman's father died, and he had no sons, so the inheritance was to go to the daughter. The relatives didn't like that and trumped up false charges, bribed someone, and had her put in jail. By the time we met she had been in jail for nearly five years and the inheritance had long been divided among her relatives.

I talked to a group of these women prisoners through a translator and asked whether any of them couldn't read Malagasy and wanted to learn. Over one-third of them quickly raised their hands. The need was strong. They wanted books and Bibles in Malagasy. They wanted clothes and nutritious food. Limited and inadequate food was provided by the prison; it was expected that the prisoners' families would provide more. Many prisoners had no family, and the families of others had forgotten them or lived too far away to help. The prison was infested with lice, fleas, and other insects, and the rats often bit the babies at night. In spite of their problems, these women prisoners were optimistic. They sang a lovely Malagasy song for us.

We were surprised to see one *vazaha* holding a tiny Malagasy baby. Her Swiss organization had been working in Madagascar for twelve years, focusing only on the babies. She had been there for one year and visited the prison every day, bringing powdered milk and feeding and holding the babies.

How can one help so many? The conditions in the prison were bad enough, but the discouraging thing was the corrupt system, within which it often took years for a case to reach trial. Even then, those with the biggest bribes won. The men were discouraged and seemed just to accept their lot; among the women, hope seemed to spring eternal—they were determined to fight for their own futures and for their children.

Lepers: "Unclean! Unclean!"

"Unclean, unclean!" How often we've read the Bible stories where lepers must announce their presence by calling out "Unclean!"

Indeed, the book of Leviticus (13:45) tells us: "The person with such an infectious disease must . . . cry out, 'Unclean! Unclean!'" In early times, leprosy was viewed as one of the most dreadful of all diseases. But could there possibly be lepers in Madagascar, as we saw in India?

We visited the Leprosy Center and Hospital, perhaps ninety minutes into the mountains outside Antananarivo, the capital. It was run by FJKM. There have long been treatments for arresting leprosy, but many cases still go untreated in Madagascar. Usually by the time a leprosy patient came to the hospital, the damage had been done. Noses were gone, fingers, toes, and entire legs and arms were disfigured or gone.

Families were disgraced when they found leprosy in any family member. Usually they'd hide the afflicted person until the village found out. Then, ashamed and helpless, the lepers found their way from faraway villages to the Leprosy Center. Some stayed for three to four months, getting the treatment, promising to continue the treatment back in their villages. Others stayed on, for while they were no longer contagious and the disease had been arrested, they knew they would not be accepted in their villages. It often takes generations to remove the fear and the stigma of leprosy.

Let me tell you about Tiana. She was eighteen years old, and the nurse said she was always sad. Tiana had been brought to the hospital from a faraway village as a toddler when her mother saw that leprosy had taken one foot and most of her fingers. By then, her mother could no longer hide her. Tiana had had the treatment, and the disease had been arrested. But her mother never returned for her. No one ever visited or even inquired about her. She couldn't read or write in Malagasy, and with no fingers she couldn't learn craft skills or do gardening. Life was indeed hard for Tiana.

Rene had only stumps for feet. It took determination and practice for her to learn to balance and walk. Another elderly woman, Yvette, had been at the center for eight years. She said she was too old to go back to her village and probably no one wanted her there anyhow. The disease had progressed too far by the time she sought treatment. She was blind and had only claws for hands and feet.

Meet Jeannine, so cheerful in spite of her many problems. Jeannine had been at the center for five years, wore an old rusty prosthesis where one entire leg was gone, and she kept her one remaining foot swathed in thick bandages. When she stuck out both hands to grab mine in greeting, I realized that she had no fingers on either hand, just rounded stumps. I knew she was married. I asked (all this through an interpreter) whether she had children. Yes, three. I told her I had two, so she had me beat. We laughed. Did she have grandchildren? Yes, twelve. I had six, so again she had me beat. More laughter.

Just as we were leaving, she told me she could write. Could she write to me? Of course—we'd get translators, and I'd send a picture. Outside her room, I commented that she probably couldn't even feed herself. Perline, my translator, stuck her head back into the room and asked Jeannine if she fed herself. Jeannine laughed and invited us back in. Her plate of rice and one sausage had just been brought in. She grabbed the plate with the stubs of her hands, put it on her lap, then putting the big spoon between her stubs, got rice and jammed it into her open mouth. She did the same with the fork, jabbing the sausage and bringing it to her mouth. I applauded. I gave a "thumbs up" and congratulated her. What an indomitable spirit!

But just as remarkable as the leper patients were the three attendants. Jeanne Rohner, an amazing French nurse who had dedicated her life to this work, had been there for over thirty years, and Dr. Nirina, a beautiful young Malagasy doctor who had been sent to the center by the Madagascar Health Department three years ago, had decided she must stay. And Pastor Herisolo continued to live here with his family.

La Maison de l'Eau de Coco

There was no starvation in Madagascar, but the pervading poverty was depressing. It gave us hope to see what one man had done in one of the poorest sections of Fianarantsoa.

Just three years before we met him, Jose Luis Guirao Pineyro, a Spanish veterinarian, was moved by the plight of the people when he visited Madagascar. Feeling that he wanted to give his life to helping people rather than animals, he started a project that he called "La Maison de l'Eau de Coco" ("The House of the Coconut Water"), with no sponsors or government aid, just himself and help from his family and friends at home.

He saw the desperate plight of women and decided to focus on them in three areas: women in prison who had no advocates or hope; adolescent girls who had turned to prostitution; and street families abandoned by their men.

Nearly thirty women prisoners in Fianarantsoa, jailed for indefinite terms with no trials or advocates, were busy working on new skills—weaving, knitting, crocheting, embroidering. When Jose Luis came to this craft center with us, the women laughed and called his name, reaching out to take his hand. Already his advocacy had overcome a few of the false charges and bribes, giving the women real hope.

In the meantime they were learning new craft skills in an abandoned warehouse behind the prison, where they had been given permission to work for up to three hours a day. Already they were earning their own money. Two-thirds of the sales income went directly to the women, one-third to Jose Luis's administrative costs.

Malagasy children were supposed to be in school for five years; in practice, they were not. Fees for books and uniforms were beyond the grasp of most. Young boys were on the streets, young girls were turning to prostitution. Jose Luis had gathered thirty-five young prostitutes who wanted to change but knew it was impossible without some support. He included them among his hundreds of street families, abandoned women and children, to make a real extended family.

Jose Luis somehow gathered enough funds to purchase two hectares of land (nearly five acres) just outside the city, and this was "home" for nearly four hundred women, adolescents, and children. It was exciting to see well-directed activities. Nearly fifty babies were napping in one covered area, their mothers nearby, washing clothes, laughing as they hung the clothes to dry. Other women were weaving sleeping mats, working in gardens, recycling old tin, supervising toddlers' games, making brooms or sewing on foot-pedaled sewing machines. Four women were in charge of feeding the "family," assigning jobs of preparing vegetables, cooking, serving, and cleaning up.

The girls and women got ten months of training—in cooking, nutrition, child care, gardening, sewing and other crafts, hygiene, and basic literacy. Always emphasized was the need for them to have skills to care for themselves and their families. If after ten months a woman proved that she could get a job with the skills she had learned, and if she had proved that she could budget her limited income, she could move to another small area, where Jose Luis, together with the newly trained women, had built tiny brick-and-stucco houses. For five thousand Malagascar francs (less than one US dollar) per month, she could rent a house. After five years, if the woman had proved she could handle herself and her family (the tiny three rooms usually housed up to eight people) and budget her limited income, the house was hers.

The positive results of Jose's programs had drawn the attention of UNICEF and German and Dutch foundations. People are willing to give generously when there is a real need, when the people being helped are actively involved, and when they see results. La Maison de l'Eau de Coco was just that kind of a program.

Most recently, Jose Luis had reopened the only old theater in Fianarantsoa. Now, with the help of overseas friends, he was bringing in classic movies. This gave work to perhaps twenty of his women, and because there was no similar theater in the entire city, it had become a popular place for Malagasy families to come with their children. It has proven to be a big success financially as well.

It was people like Jose Luis, with vision, creativity, and the willingness to work to help others, that allowed us to see *hope* in this poor, poor country.

Lemurs and the Rainforests

The island of Madagascar was once 90 percent rainforest, with an abundance of wildlife and exotic birds. Now it is less than 10 percent rainforest. Over the years, slash-and-burn agriculture has destroyed millions of trees, leaving the red clay bare, eroding the steep mountainsides into the oceans. The inhabitants continue to cut most of the remaining trees for their simple houses and for charcoal, their main source of cooking fuel.

We drove four hours east from Antananarivo, the capital, over the only paved two-lane road in the country. We drove over hills and between mountains and saw terraced rice paddies and traditional villages with thatch-roofed plaster huts, and always people walking, carrying heavy loads on their heads. The countryside was as poor as the cities.

The closer we came to Moramanga, the last small city before the Perinet Rain Forest, a national reserve, the harder it rained. But what else? This was, after all, a *rain*forest.

Our small hotel was right on the edge of the reserve, at the side of a red-dirt road in a dense grove of trees. Picturesque A-frames with thatched roofs were set in rows for those adventurous enough to visit during the rainy season. We were delighted to see netting for our beds and a flush toilet and simple shower in the back of our temporary home.

There was only one dim lightbulb, but we had our flashlights handy, for one never knew when the electricity would cut off. Because this was not the tourist season, there were only six other guests, most of them French. We joined them for a simple dinner.

Then we went off with our guide, the only one who spoke some English, to explore the after-dark life of the rainforest. He pointed a powerful flashlight at the treetops. We were looking for lemurs, the monkeylike primates that are found only in Madagascar, and for tiny half-inch tree frogs.

We listened for the lemur calls to try to locate them, then looked for their eyes, which shone like two yellow lights when the flashlight was trained on them. We saw three lemurs—tiny ones, no longer than five inches, with fat tails—and our guide found several tiny tree frogs.

It was exciting, but it was also cold and damp. We were somewhat disappointed. Was that all we'd see of lemurs? Shadows in the trees at night?

The next morning our guide met us 7 a.m. No rain—it was clear, with patches of blue sky. Soon we were off, walking carefully over the narrow, slippery path, up fairly steep inclines, among dense trees, tall exotic plants, huge ferns, and vines. We'd walk, listen, look. Our guide explained that it was difficult to see the brown, medium-sized lemurs because they travel; they don't have specific territories as other lemurs do. He spotted them first, a family of eight, light and medium brown, about fifteen inches long with long bushy tails, jumping from tree to tree and calling out to each other.

More walking, searching, listening, looking. Our guide pointed—there were four huge (over three feet tall and fat) white-and-gray lemurs, leaping from tree to tree, howling to signal us that this was *their* area. The white-and-gray lemurs are easier to find once you identify their specific territory. But it was in Toamasina, on the east coast of Madagascar, that we saw lemurs close up. In the small rainforest reserve there we watched the three-foot-tall, gray-and-white lemurs as they jumped from tree to tree above us. We glanced to our right, for we heard strange noises—and there, not more than ten feet away, were two lemurs wrestling and playing. As we stood very still, snapping photos, three more joined them. For over fifteen minutes we stood, enraptured by five gray-and-white lemurs playing joyfully just three feet away.

Beautiful, graceful creatures! How sad there wasn't more forest for these beautiful animals to breed and grow. Later, USAID people told us that plans were under way to establish corridors of rainforest to connect Madagascar's reserves so that lemurs, exotic birds, and other animal life would be able to roam across the island. They hoped this corridor would attract tourists to the amazing but diminishing land of the lemurs.

✪⁹ Cambodia, 1999

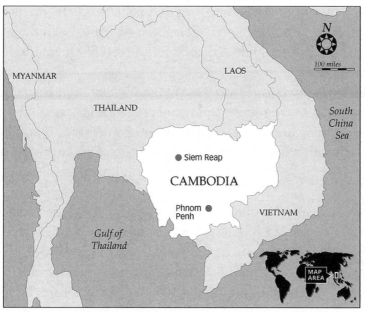

Map of Cambodia by Peter Allen.

Cambodia . . . We rode on motorbikes down narrow paths through rice paddies. We'd been told to keep to the paths, for the land on either side was still mined. We rode in trucks that were always in low gear because of the potholes, and when we came to a bridge that had been destroyed, we would drive into the water-filled gully to get across. Danger was everywhere. One teacher was returning from her village in a rented "taxi"; it overturned and two were killed, though she survived. Two other teachers couldn't fit in that taxi and had to wait for a later bus. They might have been killed, too.

Cambodia, a tiny country on the other side of the world, came to the world's attention during the dictatorship of Pol Pot, whose Khmer Rouge forces murdered millions of fellow Cambodians in the late 1970s and early 1980s. Elections in 1993 restored some semblance of democracy. Bob and I had been sent to Cambodia by ADRA (Adventist Development and Relief Agency) to give training in literacy.

The Khmer Rouge had been vanquished, but many Cambodians continued to go hungry. A woman poisoned her husband and her six children because she couldn't bear to see them starve. A woman in Kompong Thom sold a six-week-old baby in the market for ten dollars, enough to buy food for the rest of her family. Frightening stories.

Everyone had stories to tell about the Khmer Rouge era. A teacher told me that during those times, anyone with glasses threw them away; wearing them indicated that you could read, that you had some education. To survive, you had to pretend you were a peasant.

Who Are the Cambodian People?

Nearly every Cambodian home has a small statue of the Buddha in a place of honor, with offerings of flowers, food, and candles or joss sticks. Most restaurants have similar shrines, secure in the belief that daily worship will ensure success in their work.

Even more fascinating are the Buddhist spirit houses. Buddhists believe that spirits inhabit the earth and that you have displaced them from their homes when you occupy specific land areas, be it for a home, a shop, or a hotel. It's important to appease these spirits. One common way is to provide them their own "spirit house," even if it's as simple as a tin can nailed to a tree where joss sticks, flowers, and food can be offered.

Rice: One Family Trying to Survive

Rice is the basic food of Cambodians. A normal family of seven—four adults and three children—eats about 165 pounds of rice per month. That's about 1,980 pounds a year.

A traditional village family owned about two and a half acres of land. A normal yield in the poor soil of Cambodia was usually not enough for the family. To survive until the next rice harvest, many village farmers had to "borrow" rice at the end of each year.

One family we visited was very discouraged. They had worked hard, planted the rice, and harvested, husked, and dried it, but it didn't last the year. To survive, they went to a landowner to borrow rice, but the condition he set was that double the amount borrowed would have to be returned, not at the convenience of the farmer but from the first yield the following year. The family knew it would have to sell half its land and that all the family members would have to become field workers.

Death and Cambodian Customs

*An earlier version of this article appeared
in the* Syracuse Post-Standard *on August 1, 1999.*

Death rates are high in Cambodia, and every day there were funeral processions going right by our home there. Phy, my translator, invited me to accompany her to a friend's brother's funeral. We hurried along the busy street, following the mournful chanting of the monks.

The simple room was crowded with people sitting on mats on the dirt floor. I bowed my head with the others, but as I discreetly raised my eyes to look around, I noticed that all the women were wearing black and white and that all of the older women had shaved their heads bald. I had forgotten that the custom in Cambodia was for the widow to shave her head. And there were many bald women in Cambodia—all the older men had been killed during Pol Pot's rule.

Five young Buddhist monks in bright orange robes sat along the wall in lotus position, in front of a long white cloth laden with food, glasses of water, flowers, and candles, chanting in Khmer. At the far end was a picture of the young man, who had died of AIDS.

35. Buddhist monks preside at a funeral, but it also is an opportunity for them to partake of abundant food.

An elderly man, evidently a leader in the community, seemed in charge. I was introduced, and we exchanged greetings. He invited me to sit with the mourners.

After half an hour of chanting, some signal indicated that the monks could eat. They pressed the palms of their hands together, bowed their heads, repeated what I assumed was a blessing on the food, and loaded their bowls with rice and the great variety of food. Sharing food was very important, especially since the Pol Pot era, when starvation had been endemic. Monks must beg each morning for their daily food, so this abundance of food at a funeral must have been a blessing to them.

The funeral procession was led by four monks, who sat on the truck with the coffin, chanting rhythmically, beside flowers and a picture of the deceased. Family members walked behind, followed by hundreds of schoolchildren in white shirts and black skirts or trousers. Had this young man been a teacher? We learned later that it's honorable to have many mourners in a funeral procession. Schoolchildren were given new exercise books if they participated.

36. Funeral processions are common in Cambodia, for life is hard with little medical help. Long lines of mourners honor the deceased.

The family got more mourners and the children got free writing books—an "all-win" situation.

A New Baby Is Born

We shared our living quarters in Siem Reap with David, the Australian leader of our project, and his lovely Khmer wife, Khe-An, who was pregnant. What an opportunity to learn more about Cambodian customs and traditions!

Families in the Siem Reap area followed traditional birthing practices, so David and Khe-An went to Phnom Penh to have the baby. I learned much about traditional birthing. Well respected in each village were the TBAs—traditional birth attendants. Most of these women were over forty (old by Khmer standards, for life expectancy in the country is 49.7 years) and had survived the Pol Pot era. They had no formal schooling or training; all they knew about birthing had been passed down to them from their mothers and grandmothers. Much of this passed-down knowledge was practical, but many of the practices were dangerous superstitions. It's natural to resist change, and they had to be reminded again and again that Cambodia had one of the world's highest infant mortality rates: one child in ten did not survive one year.

Khe-An and David had a beautiful little girl, Kanika. We went to visit them in the hospital in Phnom Penh. After seeing what village facilities were like, we were amazed to find a new, modern hospital built by the Japanese. There were tile and marble floors, big windows, open spaces, modern beds, chairs, lovely outdoor landscaping! But we saw no doctors and only a few attendants. Most of the nursing duties were performed by family members, who were constantly in the rooms with the patients. The family was responsible for whatever medication was needed, including daily food.

Yes, life goes on—death and new life!

Pol Pot and the Killing Fields

*An earlier version of this article appeared
in the* Syracuse Post-Standard *on July 28, 1999.*

To understand the multiple problems facing Cambodia today, you need to know about the Pol Pot era, 1975 to 1979, when nearly two million Cambodians—one-quarter of the entire population—were killed by the Khmer Rouge.

Pol Pot planned to turn Cambodia into a completely self-sufficient agricultural nation modeled on the old Khmer Empire, when the peasant farmers toiled in the fields to produce wealth for the all-powerful government.

He ordered his troops to march all residents of cities and towns into the countryside to work. Those who resisted were executed, and those with any education—teachers, doctors, nurses, landowners, businessmen, monks—were killed.

The military wanted to get as much work out of the people as possible while saving its bullets for Cambodia's traditional enemy,

Vietnam. So, many were hanged, then stuffed into plastic bags and thrown into the river. Most, though, were buried in mass graves. In groups of hundreds, the starving Cambodians would be forced to dig mass graves, then remove their clothing and kneel down. Then an army officer would swing an ax and split their skulls. Thousands of split skulls have been found to verify this story—a reminder that the entire educated population of Cambodia had been killed—an entire generation lost forever.

One man, Buon, told me that he had been "killed twice." First, he had been shot, but he didn't die. Then he was one of those forced to dig a mass grave, remove his clothes, and kneel for the blow. Somehow the blow to his head did not kill him but only knocked him out. He was pushed unconscious into the open pit. It was dark when he revived, squeezed in among the corpses. He didn't dare move but waited until there were no sounds. Then he climbed over the dead bodies of his friends and out of the mass grave, and he fled.

Our secretary, ThyDa, was from an educated family. Those with glasses threw them away, and everyone pretended to be just "workers." Somehow the army found out that her brother-in-law had been a teacher. He was captured and taken to the mountains to be killed, along with his wife and their three-month-old baby.

Everyone in her family was starving—one handful of rice per day per person was the ration—so ThyDa made her decision. She became a government spy, going on daily exploring missions as she worked and starved in the local rice fields. She survived—most of her family did not.

Thousands were tortured and killed in primitive prisons, where skulls lined the walls, verifying the brutal deaths.

Everyone had a story—mothers, father, grandparents, teenagers. Khan was a teenager in the late 1970s. He was separated from his family by the Khmer Rouge army and placed with a group of boys of similar age. They were told that their parents' values were wrong; that this was the new Kampuchea, which would surpass the old Khmer Empire; and that they must seek out and inform on

37. Thousands of skulls are on display; the people want everyone to know of their tragedy, for it must never happen again.

the "bad" leaders. Khan couldn't believe these lies, but he had to pretend. The boys' main concerns? Finding enough food to keep themselves alive and searching for their lost families. Few teenagers survived.

Vanna shared with me her own story about the Pol Pot era. Her death had been ordered three times. When she was sixteen she was herded together with others who were educated. They were all to be killed. Then a female Khmer leader asked why this girl was being shot. She ordered them not to kill her. Again the next year, she was brought out to be killed with others in a mass grave. At the last minute she was spared. Then, when she was eighteen, the Vietnamese were invading. While the others ran for the forests, she stayed and was taken by the remaining Khmer Rouge, who tied her hands behind her back. They insisted that she was the one who had betrayed them to the Vietnamese, but she stood tall and told them she didn't even know herself where the Khmer Rouge were, so how could she do that? In the end, they believed her and untied her hands.

Visiting the killing fields, seeing the pits dug by the victims for their own mass graves, viewing the thousands of skulls, brought the tragic events of Cambodia's civil war home to us. Two million dead—thousands of split skulls, thousands drowned, thousands starved to death. These were not just statistics—they had been real people, each of them someone's father, mother, son, daughter.

The survivors have erected a memorial to the lost generation and have vowed that it will never again happen in Cambodia. Those survivors have been resilient. They're now grandfathers and grandmothers, working to build the newest generation of Cambodians.

Rural Cambodia from a Motorbike

To see the real Cambodia you must visit the villages, where 80 percent of Cambodians live. I traveled the country mainly on the back of a motorbike—bumpy, dusty, but exhilarating. We had been warned never to leave the paths, for the fields were still strewn with mines. I visited literacy classes held in simple buildings, and others held in a Buddhist temple, where the students sat on rugged planks at one end while monks worshipped at colorful shrines at the other.

It was in Siem Reap, in the north, that we spent most of our time. Siem Reap is a small, quiet city that adheres to traditional ways.

According to the Cambodian government, 35 percent of Cambodians are illiterate. In other words, according to the government's own definition of literacy, 65 percent are able to "read and write a simple sentence and count." That is hardly functional literacy by American standards. It is also estimated that one-third of these "literate" readers have lapsed back into illiteracy.

I could always tell how many people were attending my lessons by the number of shoes outside the door. It is the custom in Cambodia to remove one's footwear before entering any building. Before

38. Riding a motorcycle in rural Cambodia is more than an adventure—it's the only way to see real life on the back roads.

each session of my literacy training, I was met with the traditional Cambodian bow and greeting: *joam reep soor.*

The philosophy of my basic training—learning-centered, collaborative, participatory—was new to Cambodians. Their entire educational system had been based on rote learning in the ancient Khmer script—no Roman letters. So I faced quite a challenge. Most classes met in a convenient village, usually under one of the houses, with other villagers and their livestock looking on.

After two months, ten newly trained women were teaching 103 students in the villages. Most of the students were adult women who had never been to school. But will these teachers continue? And will they adapt their new classes to the needs of the village women? What a delight it was to have Lavy, one of my dedicated new teachers, come to our apartment, press her palms together, and bow "thank you" in the traditional Khmer way.

39. *The village people who gathered as their new teacher gave her first class were curious, yet hesitant.*

Have You Ever Seen a Land Mine?

Parts of this article appeared in the
Syracuse Post-Standard *on July 29, 1999.*

There were still visible signs of the land mines set by the Khmer Rouge army—disfigured men, women, and children without legs or arms. Red warning posters with a skull and crossbones reminded us that land mines were still being detected in rural areas.

Do you know what a land mine looks like? We didn't. They come in various sizes and shapes. Ben Davis, one of ADRA's project leaders, had learned how to defuse them and to use the explosives they contained to blast the rocky soil for wells.

Village children were warned not to leave the well-traveled paths, for one never knew where the mines were and it took only one blast to lose an arm or a leg. The small, green, round, three-inch explosives had been planted in rice fields, usually barely covered

40. *The skull and crossbones signs were everywhere along the village paths, reminding everyone of the mines in the fields.*

by dirt or leaves. The larger ones had been used to destroy bridges. Land mines had already killed thousands of men, women, and children and crippled thirty-five thousand more.

Most amputees survived by begging. They stood, hat in hand, displaying a stump of a leg or arm or a badly scarred face. We were told not to give money, for that only encouraged them, but it was nearly impossible to ignore their pitiful cries for help. What were the alternatives?

The Quakers were running a project where they supplied and fitted prostheses. The Maryknolls were training disabled Khmers—spinning, weaving, typing, tailoring, woodworking—and building their self-esteem. There were nearly as many polio victims in

Cambodia as there were amputees, for the country had gone twenty years with no vaccines and little medical care.

Let me share the story of Narath, a beautiful Cambodian girl, elegant in her long Khmer skirt. Narath had lost her legs when she stepped on a land mine in her village near the Mekong River. She was learning to be a tailor at the Training Center, but her colleagues were proud of her for another reason—she had won first place in a recent swimming competition for the handicapped.

Mok was probably twenty-five years old, the teacher in the new computer class. He had come to this training program from a tiny village in northern Cambodia, where he had contracted polio when he was five years old. His legs were useless, and he had no hope of being able to help with gardening or rice growing in his village. But a wheelchair gave him mobility.

He had never been to school, and first he wanted to learn to read and write Khmer, his own language. His next goal was typing, for his mind seemed to race faster than his ability to write. A donation of six computers to the center gave him opportunities to adapt to this newest technology. On his own, he mastered the basics of computers, which he then taught others.

Kim was probably twelve years old. One leg had been amputated above the knee, and the other was useless, but he smiled as he pushed his wheelchair at an incredible speed along the path. He spoke simple English, so I asked him, "A land mine?" "No," he said, "a gang." Somewhere near his village a gang of disgruntled soldiers had stolen what little he had and chopped off one leg and battered the other, leaving it useless forever.

After a grueling two months of work, I felt I deserved to relax with one of the famous Cambodian massages. Sok was blind and had suffered through many skin grafts to improve his badly disfigured face. He had been in school, hoping to become a doctor, when hoodlums came to rob him of his few possessions, throwing acid in his face to deter him. After extensive plastic surgery by foreign doctors, Sok, while still badly disfigured, is able to pursue a professional career as a masseuse, using his knowledge of the human body to be an independent and useful citizen again.

Angkor Wat

An earlier version of this article appeared in the Syracuse Post-Standard *on July 25, 1999.*

All Cambodians are intensely proud of Angkor Wat. For them it is a monument to their illustrious past and a reminder of their hope for the future. These awe-inspiring ruins have survived bitter reversals of fortune down through the centuries. The ruins, a priceless heritage, are once more accessible after long years of occupation and civil war.

Angkor Wat is a temple complex surrounded by long walls and deep, wide moats. It was built in the twelfth century as the capital of the early Khmer Empire, and it covers several square miles. The mammoth stones of the hundreds of buildings were brought

41. *Angkor Wat is the pride of all Cambodians, a reminder of their illustrious past and their hope for the future.*

to the site by barge and hauled into place by elephants, then fitted together without a seam. The main temple took thirty-seven years to build and still has its moat.

Hinduism was the religion of Cambodia at that time and is visible in the intricate bas relief sculptures of gods and warriors that cover every building. In the fourteenth or fifteenth century, Angkor Wat was abandoned to the jungle. It was "discovered" by Europeans in 1860 and is very slowly being restored. It's fascinating how over the centuries, gnarled trees and roots have intertwined with the stones of the temple complex. Long walls show huge elephants being used as beasts of burden.

In later centuries the Cambodians converted to Buddhism, and other altars and statues were brought into the temples. Even now in these ancient ruins you can see large statues of Buddha, draped in orange cloth, with people placing food and flowers and lighting joss sticks as they bow in worship.

But just as important as the architecture and religious features of Angkor Wat are the extensive canals and reservoirs. At a time when floods and droughts often brought disaster, the efficient channeling of water gave an excellent economic base, meaning better rice production for the people.

Cambodia will probably never return to the glory days of the Khmer Empire, but it can share its heritage and the ruins of its early civilization, reminding us that powerful empires and advanced civilizations can and often do tumble.

Epilogue

Bob and I recently celebrated our seventieth wedding anniversary (I am ninety-four and Bob is ninety-six), slowing down in our work but still healthy and active, working to keep a balance physically, mentally, emotionally, and spiritually.

My grandparents came to the United States, to Chicago, as teenagers from Sweden, while Bob's came from England and Germany. My father died at age thirty-eight, leaving my mother with five children: I was the oldest, twelve years old, down to my youngest sister at two, with polio. My mother had to be strong, with a lonely life with big responsibilities ahead of her. She, Lillian, our "Mom," "Gran" to everyone, was my ideal and model. Because I was the eldest, I think I've always been "grown up," and mother depended on me in many ways.

My family fell in love with Bob just as I had—he was my siblings' big brother, and we had good times together as Bob courted me. But in the late 1930s jobs were hard to get, and Bob got a job in Seattle. I suggested to my mother that perhaps we should ask him to return to Chicago because she needed me. But, no, Mom insisted that my place was in Seattle with him. She gave me the most meaningful gift, the gift of letting me go *without guilt*. She gave me roots and wings.

We lived and raised our two children in Syracuse, New York (having lived only a year and a half in Seattle). As a typical mother, I hoped both children would stay in Syracuse, but that was not to be. Terry, an economist from MIT, married Tammy, and they live in Washington, DC, where they raised their four children. Lindy, a psychotherapist, married Doug, and they live in Livermore, California, where they brought up their two children. I remembered my mother's gift, and Bob and I let them go, wishing them well, *without guilt*.

Yes, six grandchildren—but coast to coast. How could we become close to them so far away? When David, our first grandchild, was born, Bob and I set up a plan (of course with the consent of their parents)—when he was five he could fly all alone from Washington, DC, to stay a week with us. When he was seven he could come for two weeks, and when he was eleven or twelve, we'd invite him on an international trip. What we had nearly forgotten was that twelve years, which seemed so far away, does come—and that we might have more grandchildren—and that they don't forget.

When David was twelve, we were invited to Ecuador for three months; David was invited for three weeks. Brian was invited to Ecuador for our second tour of duty there. Miriam came to visit us in Turkey; Peter to Costa Rica; Karen to Harbin, northern China; and Elizabeth to Zambia, Africa. Experiences together brought us closer as well as giving them their first international experiences, living as we lived, not as tourists, but with the people.

Our children, our six grandchildren, and now our four great grandchildren, are living in different parts of the United States and Canada—but we keep in close touch by phone, by e-mails, by photos, and by occasional visits and get-togethers.

Who sent us on these various work trips? The Global Ministries of the United Methodist Church sent us to India, South Africa, and many other African countries. Bob's company, Oakite Products, Inc., also sent us to South Africa. The Rotarians of East Syracuse, New York, sent us to Nigeria, while the North East Synod of the Presbyterians (USA) sent us to Madagascar. ADRA (Adventist Development and Relief Agency) invited us to work in Papua New Guinea, Solomon Islands, and Cambodia. Two universities (Heilongjiang University in Harbin and HwaNan University in Foujou) invited us to China, and it was IESC (the International Executive Service Corps) that sent us to Turkey, Ecuador, Swaziland, and Zambia.

What is the IESC? The International Executive Service Corps is a not-for-profit organization in Stamford, Connecticut, "a global network of people working to upgrade management skills, improve basic business technologies and promote better trade relations around the world." It invites and sends retirees, as volunteers, "highly skilled U.S. executives and technical advisors to share their years of experience with businesses in the developing nations." Bob was invited (I was included as his spouse) first to Ecuador, then to Turkey. At that time only men were invited as volunteer executives working within industry, but in 1991, when IESC realized that industry needed a literate workforce, I was invited to work in Swaziland and Zambia as an IESC co-executive with Bob.

Bob is a "problem solver," basically within industry, specifically focusing on industrial chemicals and their uses. His way of "selling" is to identify and solve problems, often those costing industrial plants millions of dollars. Having located and solved their problems, they wanted to purchase the chemicals he recommended.

42. *Ruth with President Ronald Reagan when he presented her with the Presidential Medal for Volunteer Action.*

Let me tell you of his work in Turkey. Bob was invited by the IESC to help a large chemical company in Istanbul—to review their chemical formulas, to recommend which were the most effective, and to train their sales force in his "way of selling," which was never to ask for an order but just to look for problems (and every plant has problems) and solve them—the sales definitely WILL come.

The top management was convinced that Bob's way would be their way to success, and the salesmen were trained and instructed to follow Bob's instructions. All agreed except one man from Izmir. He pleaded with Bob saying, "Mister Bob, I just can't do it. I have a wife and children—we have no other income. I must ask for orders and get sales." Bob encouraged him to try, but it was when the top management insisted that the young man from Izmir knew he must do so.

After three months, it was time for us to return home. A big thank-you party was given for us by the company owners, but it was a tiny loom starting a miniature hand-made rug, with Bob's name inscribed on it, that meant most to him. It was from the young man from Izmir, who insisted that Bob had changed his way of living. Bob said, "No, I just changed your way of selling."

"Yes, that too. But when I saw that when I helped people in other plants, they wanted not only to buy my products but actually thanked me as a friend, well, I thought I'd try that at home, too. I quietly tried helping my wife and children, helping to solve THEIR problems. What happened? They then worked harder to help ME. So, thank you, Mister Bob, for helping to change my life."

And what about health problems when we're in remote out-of-the-way places?

Bob and I are highly aware of the importance of staying healthy during our travels. We can't be of much help if we get malaria or dysentery or other diseases prevalent in developing countries. So we drink only bottled water (or Coca-Cola or beer), we eat only fruit that can be peeled, we eat no fresh vegetables, and we wash our hands every chance we get.

But we have sometimes had to break these rules. In a remote village in India, a peasant woman had invited us into her modest hut for tea. She heated the water over a dung fire, but not hot enough to boil the water, only to warm it. She poured it into her best china cup—chipped and probably washed in tepid water and dusty from sitting on the shelf. Should we drink the tea, knowing there's a big chance we'll get diarrhea, or should we keep our health regimen and offend the woman? We drank the tea—luckily for us, with no ill effects.

While visiting a remote village in Cambodia, we were offered a locally bottled soft drink. We had finished the bottled water we'd brought hours ago, and with the terribly hot sun we were very thirsty. No one would be offended if we refused the bottled drink, and we had a training planned for the next day. So I said I was okay and refused the locally bottled drink, thirsty as I was.

In one of the South American countries, we felt safe drinking the water in our local hosts' home because they insisted it was safe. They forgot to tell us that the ice cubes hadn't been made with boiled water. A terrible bout of diarrhea nearly crippled us with dehydration.

In the Grand Bazaar in Istanbul, I had found the exact item of jewelry I had been looking for. Bargaining was expected, and the shop owner and I finally agreed on a price. Through our friendly bargaining, the shop owner and I had become friends, and he invited me to join him for tea. I wasn't sure the water had been boiled, so I looked at my watch, saying it was getting late, and I tried politely to excuse myself. His response—"No tea, no sale." It would have been rude of me to reject his offer, and needless to say, we had tea together. I had no ill effects, and I still cherish that piece of jewelry.

● ● ●

How do I give training when teaching basic English literacy? One must be sensitive to those we're teaching—adults who haven't had the advantage of learning to read and write are often shy and embarrassed; they have little self confidence, needing encouragement by showing them how much they have learned in a lifetime of living. Our training is always learner centered and collaborative, that is, the teacher and student working together as a team, focusing their teaching on the learner's goals.

Because people learn in different ways, I suggest four general techniques that can be adapted to students' needs and abilities, always focusing on comprehension.

1. Language Experience: encouraging students to tell of their goals, dreams or interests, writing the student's own words and teaching those words as sight words.

2. Sight words: teaching those nonphonetic words (*have, light*) and important safety words (*emergency, yield, one-way*) as sight words.

3. Phonics: teaching the sounds of all consonants; these sounds are constant.

4. Patterned words: teaching vowel sounds through patterns or families. While English is not phonetically regular, it is a patterned language. Consider the different sounds of *a* in *cat, car, call* and *came*—but the patterns of *–at, -ar, -all, -ame* are always the same.

When teaching English to those who cannot speak or understand English, I suggest starting with teaching listening skills (understanding what is said in English), followed by speaking skills (being able to respond so that one is understood), followed by teaching reading and writing in English.

When I was in Russia and China, I was totally illiterate in those languages—I could not understand or speak the language, and I could not read or write it either. If I had a choice of learning only one of the four components of language, which would I choose? I'd choose listening, so that I could understand what was being said by those around me. Then I'd choose speaking, so that I could respond. With these two skills, I could at least survive in Russian or China. Being able to read and write would follow as soon as possible.

What about other languages that *are* phonetically regular? Language Experience can be an excellent tool to instill confidence and ensure student participation in a first lesson in a student's native language. But those personal sight words are not enough—they must learn the sounds of the letters as well. I suggest teaching using syllables based on subjects familiar to the students. Native language books can focus on familiar, nonthreatening subjects—family, markets, health, jobs, school—using illustrations to depict the key words, encouraging discussion (remember, they CAN speak and understand the language—their problem is reading and writing it). Most of us can't understand a life without reading—not only for pleasure, but for safety, for health, for jobs. Millions of people around the world are unable to read and write the language they speak. Giving children the gift of reading can indeed break the cycle of illiteracy, but who is the child's first teacher? The mother or the father. Teaching parents can often bring an entire family to literacy, for instead of insisting that their children help them work in the fields, they see a brighter future for them and insist they stay in school.

We were always amazed that in most developing countries, the people wanted to learn English, even those who were illiterate in their own spoken language. I tried to encourage them to learn to read and write first in their native language, but because they had lived a life without reading, they understood only that learning English would get them better jobs. Research and experience, however, suggest that it's most difficult for those who cannot read and write in their first, their native language, to learn a second language. Not for everyone, of course—but for most. Why not then learn basic native language literacy as a first step to learning that second language (in this case, English)?

How did I manage language differences? An early visit to Ecuador for the IESC convinced me of the importance of knowing the language of the country where one works. I knew some Spanish, and it was amazing how quickly I was able to communicate—not in technical terms, but in basic people-to-people terms. We made friends, and Ecuadorians accepted us often just because they knew we were trying hard to communicate in *their* language.

Our next assignments, to South Africa, Turkey, and China, made me realize that it would be impossible for me to be able to communicate in a new language each year. That's when I knew I'd have to work through translators. But I soon learned how important it was to have a translator who not only translated my words, but also understood and translated my thoughts and my suggestions.

In most countries, the translators were outstanding. I learned that they don't generally translate word for word, sentence by sentence. Rather the best translators for my work were those who had me "speak in paragraphs" and then translated the whole paragraph, fitting it into the cultural patterns of that country. I tested them one time when my paragraph seemed much longer than the one they translated—I inserted a simple joke. Would she include that? I knew that she did because the trainees laughed heartily.

My major translator in Cambodia was outstanding, but at one training session, when she was unable to attend, I had to use a Khmer speaker who was against any kind of local work—she represented the government and wanted government teachers only. It was only when one of the bilingual trainees came up to me at tea time, telling me that the translator wasn't translating MY words but was criticizing my work, that I knew the importance of a reliable translator.

Because of the tremendous illiteracy problem and the great interest in learning English in most developing countries, we had no problem attracting students. They were so anxious to learn that they were willing to attend classes anywhere. Often we had trainings in huts, under the trees, and once in a part of a Buddhist worship area. Our problem was limiting the number of students our new trainees could handle with success. The new teachers were so dedicated, they wanted to take everyone. I encouraged them to limit their new classes to ten at first. After they'd had a year's experience, they would be free to decide for themselves how many they could teach with a fair amount of success.

Because of the limited education in so many developing countries, I insisted that my trainees have at least an eighth-grade education to become effective teachers. But that wasn't always possible—often I had trainees with two years of education. I soon learned that years of schooling is only *one* way of assessing qualifications of future teachers. Life experiences are most important, as well as dedication, love of learning, and the discipline to stick to an assigned task.

43. *President George W. Bush presenting Ruth with the Presidential Medal of Freedom. Photograph used with the permission of AP Images.*

We look back on our travels to sixty-two countries, especially those twenty-six developing countries where we worked. We were the minority. We were the older generation. We were often from a different faith or religion. We had to learn new customs and traditions. We are so thankful to the many friends we made; they accepted us, often including us in family gatherings—what warm hospitable people.

I hope by reading *Off the Beaten Path* you'll agree that we are indeed one world, that while we want to continue to share, we have much to learn from other countries.

Friendship Circle

I have made friends everywhere I have taught. When finishing a training, I suggest we stand in a circle, each putting the palm of the left hand *up* and the palm of the right hand *down*, and then join hands. In that way we are supporting the person on our left and being supported by the person on our right.

We sometimes just stand in silence for a few minutes. Another time we might sing (often in the local language) the old Girl Scout song, "Make New Friends":

> Make new friends but keep the old.
> One is silver and the other gold.

Then we squeeze—either all together, or I start by squeezing my left hand which supports my neighbor, who passes it on until it comes full circle.

"Amen" (meaning "So be it") or "Peace with you"—seals our friendships.

Afterword

How can you, as an individual, become an "instrument of peace"? You may or may not be able to travel and meet people of different cultures and belief systems, with customs so different from your own. But know that these same people live right in your own city and community. Would you like to meet and get to know some of them? And would it really make a difference if you met them and made new friends? Most of us tend to think of the world's problems as so big, so complex, that there's little if anything we as individuals can do.

At one time when I was on the International Center Syracuse board, we were discussing the value of hosting visitors to the United States from other countries. The National Director told us that 33 of the presidents or prime ministers of other countries, and 379 of their cabinet officers, had at one time or another visited our country, either as students or as vacationers. In other words, they had all met some Americans, and their experiences were surely affecting their decisions today. We can only hope these experiences had been good.

But some of those experiences, we know, had not been good. I understand that one of the top men in a country hostile to the United States had at one time been a student in America. He had received no invitations to American homes, had seen little of American family life, had seen no Americans helping other Americans, had seen only negative sides of America. No matter how hard American diplomats tried to reach this leader, to explain American ways, to try to help him understand our global goals of peace and friendship, it was nearly impossible. If, yes, just if, his experiences in America had been different; if he had been in several American homes to talk, to see for himself; *if* he had been included as a friend on a picnic or at a community event; *if* he had seen American volunteer efforts—Americans helping Americans; *if* he'd had even one American close enough to express his doubts, his concerns; yes, *if* the experience of just one man had been different, it just might have changed a bit of history.

You can call your own city's version of the International Center, or your local college, or your own refugee center, and invite immigrants or international students to your home for lunch or dinner, just to get acquainted and learn from each other. What better way for your children to have their first international experience!

The United States is a land of immigrants. Except for the American Indians, we all are immigrants or descendants of immigrants. And immigrants continue to come to America. Many cannot speak or understand English. Someone probably helped your ancestors learn English. Would you like to "pass it on" and teach some English?

There are local programs in many communities where you can tutor someone from another country, children and adults for whom English is a new language. Can you imagine the frustration any newcomer would feel trying to learn in a language that is so new to them?

ProLiteracy has nearly one thousand affiliates in the United States. They need volunteers and can train you to teach basic literacy or English as a second language. Just look in the phone book or on the Internet and you'll receive a warm welcome. You'll find real joy in helping someone on a one-on-one basis, and in the process you'll not only make a new friend, but you'll learn about one new country, about one newcomer, and that newcomer will learn more about America through you. One on one, but multiplied by hundreds, thousands, even by millions, we *can* make a difference!

Yes, it's lifelong learning, and what have I learned from my travels? I have learned about traveling—by airplane (747s and two-seaters), by train (fast and modern or an old steam engine), by bus (long-distance coach and a local service carrying hens and goats with the people), by bicycle or motorbike (pedaling ourselves or in rickshaws), and on foot (in developing country markets, on trash-strewn streets, and across mine-strewn fields).

I have learned about geography—mountains, plains, forests, crowded cities, remote backlands—and I have seen that a country's reality has little to do with what it looks like on a map.

I have learned about different religions (there are similarities if you look for them), about unknown customs and traditions (they somehow make sense when you're there), about fabulous wealth and extreme poverty (life isn't fair).

But most of all, I have learned about people—wonderful, caring, sharing people. No one country has a monopoly on "good people" or on "bad people"—we all have our share. But working together, we *can* live in peace.